Trends in Organizational Behavior

Volume 1

Cary L. Cooper

Currently Professor of Organizational Psychology and Deputy Chairman of the Manchester School of Management at the University of Manchester Institute of Science and Technology, Professor Cooper is the author of over 60 books (on stress, women at work, and industrial and organizational psychology), has written over 250 articles for academic journals, and is a frequent contributor to national newspapers, TV, and radio. Founding President of the British Academy of Management, he is currently Editor-in-Chief of the *Journal of Organizational Behavior*, and a Fellow of both the British Psychological Society and Royal Society of Arts.

Denise M. Rousseau

Professor of Organization Behavior at Northwestern University, Professor Rousseau received her doctorate in Industrial/Organizational Psychology from the University of California at Berkeley. Her research interests include psychological contracts, strategic human resource management, and organizational culture. Her research has appeared in prominent academic journals, such as *Journal of Applied Psychology*, *Academy of Management Review*, *Academy of Management Journal*, and *Administrative Science Quarterly*, and she is an author of the book *Developing an Interdisciplinary Science of Organizations*. She is a Fellow of both the American Psychological Association and the Society for Industrial/Organizational Psychology and is an Associate Editor of the *Journal of Organizational Behavior*.

Trends in Organizational Behavior

Volume 1

Edited by

Cary L. Cooper

Manchester School of Management, University of Manchester Institute of
Science and Technology, UK

and

Denise M. Rousseau

Kellogg School of Management, Northwestern University, USA

JOHN WILEY & SONS

Chichester · New York · Brisbane · Toronto · Singapore

Trends in Organizational Behavior, Volume 1

Published as a supplement to the
Journal of Organizational Behavior, Volume 15

Other Wiley Editorial Offices

John Wiley & Sons, Inc., 605 Third Avenue,
New York, NY 10158-0012, USA

Jacaranda Wiley Ltd, 33 Park Road, Milton,
Queensland 4064, Australia

John Wiley & Sons (Canada) Ltd, 22 Worcester Road,
Rexdale, Ontario M9W 1L1, Canada

John Wiley & Sons (SEA) Pte Ltd, 37 Jalan Pemimpin #05-04
Block B, Union Industrial Building, Singapore 2057

British Library Cataloguing in Publication Data

A catalogue record for this book is available from the British Library

ISBN 0-471-94344-4

Typeset in 10/12pt Palatino by Mackreth Media Services, Hemel Hempstead, Herts
Printed and bound in Great Britain by Biddles Ltd, Guildford, Surrey

Contents

Contributors

Julian Barling
Department of Psychology, Queen's University, Kingston, Ontario K7L 3N6, Canada.

Jeanne M. Brett
J. L. Kellogg Graduate School of Management, Northwestern University, Evanston, Illinois 60208, USA.

Sue Cartwright
Manchester School of Management, University of Manchester Institute of Science and Technology, Manchester M60 1QD, UK.

Cary L. Cooper
Manchester School of Management, University of Manchester Institute of Science and Technology, Manchester M60 1QD, UK.

Robert J. House
Wharton School of Business, University of Pennsylvania, Philadelphia, Pennsylvania 19104, USA.

Maddy Janssens
Katholieke Universiteit of Leuven, Toegepaste Economische Wetenschappen, 3000 Leuven, Belgium.

Deborah L. Kidder
Industrial Relations Center, University of Minnesota, 537 Management and Economics Building, 271 19th Avenue, South Minneapolis, Minnesota 55455, USA.

Judi McLean Parks   Industrial Relations Center, University of
                               Minnesota, 537 Management and
                               Economics Building, 271 19th Avenue,
                               South Minneapolis, Minnesota 55455, USA.

Karlene H. Roberts   College of Business Administration,
                               University of California, Berkeley,
                               California 94270, USA.

Ivan T. Robertson   Manchester School of Management,
                               University of Manchester Institute of
                               Science and Technology, Manchester
                               M60 1QD, UK.

Denise M. Rousseau   J. L. Kellogg Graduate School of
                               Management, Northwestern University,
                               Evanston, Illinois 60208, USA.

Lynn McFarlane Shore   Department of Management and W. T.
                               Beebe Institute of Personnel and
                               Employment Relations, Georgia State
                               University, Georgia 30303, USA.

Lois E. Tetrick   Department of Psychology, Wayne State
                               University, Detroit, Michigan 48202, USA.

Editorial Introduction

There are a plethora of books which provide comprehensive reviews of research on topics in industrial and organizational psychology and behavior, from the *Annual Review of Psychology* to the *International Review of Industrial and Organizational Psychology* to the *Handbook of I/O Psychology* to *Research in Organizational Behavior*. These volumes in different ways attempt to provide thorough and up-to-date accounts of research on particular topics or themes or methodological issues. Because of their need to survey an entire subject area (i.e. motivation, personnel selection), they tend to concentrate on topics where there is substantial literature rather than focus on newly emerging fields, with the inevitable consequence that the massive literature reviewed submerges some interesting gem of research or material that might be of great importance to the wider public/private sector or practitioner constituency in organizational behavior and change. In other words, there is a gap in the literature in providing short, sharp accounts of research and practice which are published quickly and represent leading trends in organizational behavior (OB). This is the purpose of this volume and all those that will follow in this annual series. Although traditional topics of motivation, leadership, job design, personnel selection, etc., will be explored (probably in terms of a specific sub-topic issue), new and more innovative OB research toward issues reflecting the increasing interdependence in organizations (between persons, across groups and between work and homelife) will be primarily highlighted. Each short chapter will be a stand-alone topic, and there will be no attempt to integrate them into theme—in a sense, the *Trends* volumes will be like a TV magazine program, with different up-to-date issues explored in a short, hopefully incisive way and published immediately—a kind of straight "off the press" OB research item.

In this first volume, we have collected together some leading OB researchers to focus on some innovative issues. Karlene Roberts explores the functional and dysfunctional linkages between organizations. For example, in terms of dysfunctional consequences, she examines incidents such as the Exxon Valdez and Chernobyl to highlight inter-organizational relationships—a phenomenon that has not really been adequately explored by OB researchers, but will in the future. Another first comes from Denise Rousseau and Robert House, who explore the grey area between micro-OB and macro-OB, or what they term "meso-OB". They contend that this third paradigm will be more integrative and organizational based, and provide the next generation context for OB research, or at least should. Maddy Janssens and Jeanne Brett provide a focus on the global company. As mergers and acquisitions increase, these global organizations are emerging from worldwide recession. They explore a variety of ways in which global companies have coordinated their activities, through electronic voice and data networks, abandonment of internal labor markets and multi-cultural management teams. Since many of these global companies are emerging from mergers and acquisitions, Sue Cartwright and Cary Cooper provide a framework for examining successful and unsuccessful marriages. They explore the ideas of open, traditional and modern/collaborative marriages in terms of organizational cultures, as well as the impact of these strategic alliances on individual employees' health and satisfaction. All the issues at work, whether of mergers/acquisitions or global mobility or organizational linkages, impact not only the individual but also the family. Julian Barling provides a set of hypotheses about the link between work and the family, testing our basic assumptions. For example, he contends that "the quality of work, rather than the amount or timing of work, is critical to understanding the balance between work and the family". In other words, it is not just long working hours that damages families but the quality of what happens at work. Many more of these types of assumptions are explored in this piece. As well as organization-wide and global issues are problems of selecting the "right person for the right job". Here, Ivan Robertson explores the role of personality assessment in personnel selection and provides a framework for looking at the personality–performance link. This leads on to Lynn Shore and Lois Tetrick's exploration of the psychological contract as an explanatory framework in the employment relationship. This chapter explores the meaning and function of the psychological contract, different types of contracts and the implications of their violation. And finally, Judi McLean Parks and Deborah Kidder examine the changing work relationships in the 1990s. They assess the impact of "a more contingent and overworked workforce", and what this means for organizational role behaviour, organizational contracts and justice at work.

We hope this telegraphic approach to OB issues will stimulate discussion and be useful to both researchers and practitioners alike, and we look forward to providing you with more "food for conceptual thought".

CLC
DMR
January 1994

CHAPTER 1

Functional and Dysfunctional Organizational Linkages

Karlene H. Roberts

University of California, Berkeley, USA

As often as they can find them journalists write about organizations which have gone amok and done great harm to themselves and their environments. Yet, until the 1980s organizational scholars had not examined this kind of organization in great detail. In the 1980s several organizational writers became interested in such organizations. Two notable contributions were Charles Perrow's book, *Normal Accidents* (1984), which chronicles a series of organization debacles, and Paul Shrivastava's (1987) analysis of the Union Carbide plant disaster at Bhopal. Other works also appeared (e.g. Bowman & Kunreuther, 1988; Kovach & Render, 1987; Moorhead, Ference & Neck, 1991; Starbuck & Milliken, 1988; Vaughan, 1990).

Other organizational researchers began to look both at organizations in which great harm had come (e.g. Weick, 1990; Roberts & Moore, 1993) and at organizations that have the capacity to foul themselves and their environments but which had not, at least at the time they were analyzed (e.g. Roberts, 1990; Roberts, Stout & Halpern, in press; Weick, 1987).

Issues of mutual interest to these researchers include concern for whether organizations that manage potentially dangerous technologies can manage without breakdown, how they are organized, and what steps these organizations take to mitigate error. During the 1980s and early 1990s a few issues were raised, some answers addressed some of these issues, and many questions were raised that are still unanswered.

Trends in Organizational Behavior, Volume 1. Edited by C. L. Cooper and D. M. Rousseau
© 1994 John Wiley & Sons Ltd.

Perrow argues that some of the organizations he examined should be shut down altogether because of the probability of risk in them, and because of the totalitarian regimes required to avoid catastrophe in them. Other authors (e.g. Roberts, 1990; Weick, 1987; Weick & Roberts, 1993) argue that society is not going to shut down nuclear power generation plants and advanced weapons systems. An illustration of this is the Bulgarian government's operation of its nuclear power plant in Kozloduy, said by experts to be the worst-run nuclear power plant in the world (Anonymous, 1990). The plant supplies 40% of Bulgaria's electricity. Bulgaria has no other means to supply that power and no money to buy it from her neighbors.

Very few authors have been concerned about requirements for mitigating disaster in these organizations. Obviously, attention to safety should be paramount and indeed several authors focus on safety as a part of the organization's culture (e.g. Koch, 1993; Schulman, 1993; Wise, 1989). Schulman (1993) provides a detailed discussion of how three reliability enhancing organizations approach the safety issue. Others (e.g. Roberts, Rousseau & La Porte, in press) describe the distinctive cultural characteristics of reliability-enhancing organizations.

Another issue receiving a small amount of attention in both reliability enhancing organizations and in organizations in which disasters have occurred is how decisions come to be made in them. Several authors address this issue in organizations involved in catastrophes. With regard to the disaster of the space shuttle, Challenger, Moorhead et al, found that groupthink properties operated in the launch decision. They amend groupthink by adding the role of time and leadership to a revised groupthink perspective. Schwartz (1987) identified a fantasy at the center of NASA's organizational processes that perceived the organization and its top managers as perfect. This contributed to lower level managers making risky decisions and reduced decision making to a ritual. Starbuck and Milliken (1988) indicated that past successes and acclimatization alter decision-makers' perceptions about the probability of future success. It appears that managers at Morton Thiokol and NASA accepted the hypothesis that success makes subsequent success appear more likely and failure makes subsequent success appear less likely. Thus, NASA fine tuned its inherently flawed system until failure occurred. In his analysis of the Tenerife airport disaster in which a KLM and a Pan Am 747 collided and 583 lives were lost, Weick (1990) indicates that stress contributed to the loss of complex responses and the return to less complicated, older, more basic responses that were inappropriate to the situation.

On the other side of the coin Roberts, Stout and Halpern (1993) examined decision making in two high reliability military organizations, which had operated potentially dangerous technologies safely over a long period of time. They found the almost simultaneous operation of centralized and decentralized decision making. Important decisions are constantly moved both up and down these organizations. The need for accuracy and high accountability of decision makers powers this fluctuation.

All of this research concentrated on behavior in single organizations or when it did consider more than one organization, as in the work of Shrivastava, Starbuck and Milliken, and Weick, it made no effort to address linkages among organizations. Yet it is clear from the nature of some organizational traumas that a significant part of their stories have to do with interdependent activities in other organizations.

In one of the few pieces in the organizational literature that begins to think about organizational relationships that can lead to serious trouble, Mitroff and Mohrman (1986) discuss the significance of what happened during a run on Savings and Loan institutions in Ohio. The fate of these organizations was tied to that of an obscure securities firm in Florida and the value of British oil stocks was linked to both. They point out that contemporary managers need to develop holistic or systems views of their organizations. In doing so, managers are getting no help from organizational scholars.

When one thinks about this it soon becomes clear that systems of organizations are linked with one another in different ways from those posed by institutional theory, agency theory, transaction cost economics, resource dependency theory, or the networking approach (Perrow, 1986). Most studies of networking in organizations examine networks within single organizations (e.g. Bush & Frohman, 1991; Shrader, Lincoln & Hoffman, 1989).

The notion of sets of organizations has been around for some time (Evan, 1966). In 1979 and again in 1986 Perrow called for using the network methodology to study the pushes and shoves on organizations that may result from forces about which they are little conscious. He noted that only one study existed that did this (Warren, Rose & Bergunder, 1974). Interestingly this study did not apply the methodological techniques of the usual network analyses. Miles and Snow (1986) and others (e.g. Nelson, 1991; Wholey & Huonker, 1993) use the language of networking, but their discussions of inter-organizational networks largely assume that the organizations involved consciously contract or otherwise build these interactions. Yet, as in Mitroff and Mohrmon's example, in some cases it is unclear that actions in one organization consciously take other organizations into consideration, but it is clear that these actions can have disastrous consequences for some organizations. Three other examples point out some of the different kinds of linkages that occur among groups of organizations.[1]

Roberts and Moore (1993) provide a case study of the Exxon Valdez accident in Prince William Sound in March, 1989. Their sources for this work were archival supplemented with interviews of members of the marine industry. Theirs is an unfolding analysis of management processes operating (or failing to operate) with pilotage, at the Coast Guard, aboard the Exxon Valdez and at Exxon Shipping Company before and at the time of the Exxon Valdez misfortune. One example of what occurred is that the organizations involved appear to have atrophied over the years since oil had begun being transited out of the port in 1977 (Davidson, 1990). The marine pilots had reduced pilotage requirements, the ship operated with two mariners on the bridge, and the Coast Guard had reduced the force in Vessel Traffic Services (VTS) over the years.

Roberts and Moore focus on the organizational processes of culture, training, and requisite variety. They make no attempt to link the organizations. However, it strongly appears that happenstance in one organization involved in this incident was not independent of happenstance in other organizations, although their members acted as though it was. For example, watch changes took place at approximately the same time at the VTS and aboard the ship. Vigilance from either location could well have avoided the accident. However, if the participants in various organizations do not understand that they are hooked together they cannot develop management policies sensitive to operating in an interdependent fashion across organizations. The organizations involved in this situation seemed to have been only superficially linked at the local level. Except for Exxon Shipping Company, they all coexisted in a horizontal plane within the same port.

That this example comes from the marine industry is particularly interesting because various factions in the industry perceive themselves as operating independently. The marine pilots, for example, are contacted by the ship's agents and perceive they will go aboard the ship as it comes close to land in order to assist the master. The master is the final authority and sees himself as operating independently of even the pilots. And the shipping companies do not perceive themselves as having a great deal to do with the Coast Guard's VTS. VTS is only advisory in this industry which is not like the function of air traffic controllers in the air transportation industry.

But as ports become more complex in their operations, there will probably have to be greater interaction among the various parties in the

---

[1] Networking has a variety of other meanings in the organizational literature.

port than was true in Prince William Sound. The port of Rotterdam, which is among the busiest ports in the world, for example, has already moved to make violation of VTS instructions punishable, therefore tightening the interdependence of the user with VTS. Other organizations are also in the process of becoming more interdependent.

The second example is taken from Piers Paul Read's account of the meltdown at the Soviet power plant at Chernobyl (Read, 1993). While Roberts and Moore describe a horizontal system in which organizations operating simultaneously in a relatively horizontal plane fail, Read discusses a vertical system in which the accident at Chernobyl is rooted in a vast system of Soviet mentality (particularly a mentality of secretiveness) that produced a number of organizations that ultimately generated the accident.

In designing the power station at Chernobyl the axiom, "the bigger the better", was put to full use. Each of the six units in the plant was to have enormous generating capacity, and the plant would be the largest in the world. The reactor was designed by the Scientific Research Institute of Technical Energy Construction (NIKYET). Given the difficulties the Soviets had faced with developing newer reactors, these designers reverted to an old reactor design that had proved so safe and reliable there seemed no need for an expensive containment structure. The major difference between the reactors at Chernobyl and other similar reactors was size. While the design used at Chernobyl was tried and true, the simple expedient of increasing its size resulted in an engineering project of enormous proportions. This enormous size worried some of the institute scientists and in 1976 one person suggested the addition of extra boron control rods to improve safety. The modification was never made. "Like so many other measures during this period, which was to be called the era of stagnation, the idea travelled sluggishly through the clogged arteries of the obese Soviet administration, moving from department to department and committee to committee in the vast bureaucracies of the NIKYET and the Ministry of Medium Machine Building". (Read, 1993, p. 16.)

The framework for the development of this reactor and nuclear power in the Soviet Union was based on deliberations by the Central Committee, the military high command, and the Ministry of Medium Machine Building. These debates were embedded in the Soviet history of nuclear development and focused on cost. Safety was never an issue. This despite the fact that there was a catastrophic accident in 1957 at Mayak in which more than 10 000 people were evacuated and 250 000 acres of agricultural land laid to waste. Two further accidents happened at Mayak and all were hidden from the outside world. "No one broke the code of *omerta*. It was not just the fear of the KGB but the esprit de corps of those who worked for the military–industrial complex.... Patriotism, too, played its part. Few doubted their government's propaganda that the Americans were preparing for war to obliterate the new Socialist civilization". (Read, 1993, p. 11.) When the accident at Three Mile Island happened in 1977, the Soviets widely believed that the Capitalist Americans were only interested in profit, not the safety of their people.

When construction of the power station was begun at Chernobyl, its manager had the awesome responsibility of supervising the building of both the power station and the town of Pripyat. The parts specified by designers were frequently impossible to find and had to be built in workshops on site. This encouraged a spirit of improvisation which was dangerous when it came to nuclear power. In addition, many of the goods obtained from other organizations were shoddy, reflecting a spirit of low concern for quality in those organizations.

The plant manager reported both to the Ministry of Medium Machine Building and to the Communist party, which acted as shadow administration in every social, political, industrial or cultural structure. One's work prospects depended on standing in the party. In 1975 there was a meltdown of a fuel element in the Number One unit in Leningrad, which was identical to the units at Chernobyl. Because of the secrecy surrounding anything to do with nuclear power the accident was concealed even from those who worked in the industry. Knowing only what they were told by their superiors or had read in the press about the absolute safety of Soviet reactors, none of the operators at Chernobyl had the opportunity to learn from the mistakes of others.

Finally, there was a dearth of experienced engineers. Many of the specialists came to the plant straight from universities and polytechnics. They had learned the theory behind nuclear power generation and certain basic skills, and they had also been taught conformity and respect for authority. They had not been encouraged to show initiative or display a spirit of inquiry. They did not have access to training on simulators, available to nuclear operators in the West.

Reactor Number Four was commissioned on 21 December, 1983. Getting the reactor commissioned at this time meant operations were a year ahead of schedule, and everyone involved would be eligible for numerous rewards. On 27 March the following year it went into commercial operation, three months ahead of schedule. The accident happened on 26 April, 1986.

Like the interdependence found in many organizations this is a story of interdependence rooted historically in ideology and the historical behavior of other organizations. The power station at Chernobyl was not only linked back to its historical roots in the Soviet approach to nuclear power, but was also linked to suppliers of shoddy material, and educational sources that failed to train people to question the viability of behaviors in their organizations. Because of the way Read tells the story we can get some glimpse of the linkages both horizontally to other organizations and back in time to "higher authority". Again, there are important lessons for managers to be learned from someone uncovering these linkages. If they had been sorted out for him perhaps the Chernobyl power station manager could have taken some steps to allay disaster. As it was he was probably like the proverbial fish who is unaware of the water so important to his existence.

The third example comes from the United States Navy. Since World War II the aircraft carrier has been the centerpiece of the Navy's fighting capacity. The carrier itself is over 1000 feet long, carries 5600 men (organized into ship's company and the air wing), and seven different types of aircraft, organized into nine squadrons. Thus, the carrier itself is several organizations. In addition, the carrier is escorted by approximately 10 support ships (cruisers, frigates, submarines, and supply ships) carrying another 2400 people, called the carrier battle group (CVBG). Often several CVBGs operate together.

Until the 1970s warfare commanders (admirals) single handedly operated their battle groups, resulting in a highly inflexible and centralized system of organization. By the mid 1970s the problem of integration resulted in the need for a different kind of system. Composite Warfare Command (CWC) was developed as a system tool to integrate up to four carrier battle groups, or about 40 ships, 320 aircraft, and 32 000 men at sea plus shore side support of another 23 400 people (US Department of the Navy, 1985).

The CWC system is designed along functional lines; under the CWC commander are various warfare commanders and coordinators. The CWC commander may give warfare commanders tactical control of resources so they can autonomously initiate action. Under the CWC's Officer of Tactical Command (OTC) are the anti-air warfare commander (AAWC), the anti-surface warfare commander (ASUWC), the anti-submarine warfare commander (ASWC), and the air element (AEWC) and electronic warfare (EWC) coordinators. For each job function there are primary and alternate roles, which designs redundancy into the system. Warfare commanders bargain with one another for assets (e.g. frigates, airplanes, submarines, etc.). For example, because of the flexibility of the E2-C Hawkeye aircraft in electronic surveillance, monitoring aircraft, etc., all the battle commanders want use of it.

The CWC concept allows the OTC to delegate tactical command to wage combat operations but retains close control over power projection and strategic sea control operations. The way duties are delegated establishes at the highest level the management principle the Navy wants to tumble down the organization: "command by negation", a strategy for allowing people to unfold their jobs without continuous direction from the top. The strategy is designed to underwrite and support the organization's attempt to maintain the "big picture", or the "bubble" (intelligence about the ongoing operation at the top of the organization) and to maintain as much of the bubble as possible at each successive level in the organization.

At the local level the organizational form duplicates that seen above in its simultaneous requirement for control and flexibility. As previously mentioned, the carrier, for example, is functionally split into ship's company and the air wing. Both the carrier air wing commander and the ship's commanding officer report to the CWC commander. Ashore both the ship and air wing maintain certain separate services (food and maintenance). Aboard ship these units merge and ship department heads and air wing staff bargain with one another for resources. This type of organizational structure allows the CWC to maintain tight control of the system during certain times and relinquish control to the local level at other times (Hughes, 1986).

The carrier itself has functional departments (e.g. Training, Maintenance, etc.) and these functional departments are mirrored by many of the same functions at the squadron level. Thus, the entire system is like a set of Chinese boxes in which the larger unit encompasses the smaller and each is mirrored in the other.

Unlike the other two examples presented here operation of this system has not yet failed. Unlike the other two systems most operations of this system have been to practice for an imagined reality. However, the Gulf War in 1991 provided an opportunity to test the system in a real situation and it worked pretty much as designed (personal correspondence, Rear Admiral Lyle Bien).

Unlike the other two systems this system is neither horizontal as was the Exxon Valdez system, nor is it rooted in the same kind of deep vertical and horizontal historical ideological system as was Chernobyl. It is a nested hierarchy designed as sequentially centralized and decentralized. Are characteristics of self destruction inherent in this system as they were in the other two systems? We have no way to know the answer. We do know that its history to date is one of successful operation. But that is also the history to date of systems that will fail tomorrow.

Because organizational studies of systems of organizations are missing, we do not have a vocabulary for discussing systems in organizational research, conceptual notions about the kinds of systems that can and cannot work, or advice to give managers who must operate in systems of organizations. It appears that here we have at least three different kinds of systems. There are probably others.

Based on our brief description of these three systems can we draw conjectures about what might and might not work? One thing that is clear is that the system in which Chernobyl was embedded was rigid and inflexible. Composite Warfare Command, on the other hand, was built with flexibility in mind. It appears that the horizontal system in which the Exxon Valdez was embedded was only loosely connected and lacked vigilance. Composite Warfare Command was designed with redundancy in vigilance, in mind. Beyond this we know too little about the organizational behavior of systems to say anything definitive.

Why do we not have an organizational behavior of systems of related organizations, particularly in light of the fact that massive organizational accidents happen to organizations embedded in environments with other organizations? The simple answer is, it's too big. A second answer is that because of the academic reward system most organizational researchers select problems and methodologies that are of limited scope. And a growing number never enter the organizations they study. The minimum requirements in studying organizational systems of trying to get a grasp on system composition, the problems involved in entry alone, and the time required to understand a system, are more than can be dealt with and meet tenure and other promotional requirements.

There are yet other reasons why systems of organizations are not studied. The boundary problems are significant enough in "normal" organizational research. They could be insurmountable in studying systems of organizations. In their discussion of the "boundaryless" company, Hirschhorn and Gilmore (1990) note the need to design more flexible organizations. They maintain that once traditional boundaries of hierarchy and function disappear new boundaries will emerge. According to these authors four new important boundaries are (1) authority, (2) task, (3) political, and (4) identity.

Finally, the complexity that we will encounter in studying systems is fearful. How will we describe them? How will we conceptualize them? How will we measure them? There are no answers. But in her intriguing book, Margaret Wheatley states:

> But there is a way out of this fear of complexity, and we find it as we step back and refocus our attention on the whole. When we give up myopic attention to details and stand far enough away to observe the movement of the total system, we develop a new appreciation for what is required to manage a complex system. Peter Senge, in his work in systems theory (1990) develops complex nonlinear systems to portray the dynamics of an organization. This whole system view requires very different management expectations and analytic processes. Rather than creating a model that

forecasts the future of the system, nonlinear models encourage the modeler to play with them and observe what happens. Different variables are tried out "in order to learn about the system's critical points and its homeostasis", Senge reports. *Controlling* the model is neither a goal nor an expectation. Analysts want to increase their intuitions about how the system works so they "can interact with it more harmoniously" (in Briggs & Peat, 1989, p. 175). (Wheatley, 1992, p. 110.)

It might be worth a try!

REFERENCES

Anonymous (1990) Nuclear morning. *New Scientist*, **128,** 1740.

Briggs, J. & Peat, F. D. (1989) *Turbulent Mirror: An Illustrated Guide to Chaos Theory and the Science of Wholeness.* New York: Harper and Row.

Bush, J. B. & Frohman, A. L. (1991) Communication in a "network" organization. *Organizational Dynamics*, **20,** 23–26.

Bowman, E. & Kunreuther, H. (1988) Post Bhopal behavior at a chemical company. *Journal of Management Studies*, **25,** 387–482.

Davidson, A. (1990) *In the Wake of the Exxon-Valdez.* San Francisco, Ca: Sierra Club.

Evan, W. M. (1966) The organization-set: Toward a theory of interorganizational relations. In J. D. Thompson (Ed.) *Approaches to Organizational Design.* Pittsburgh: University of Pittsburgh Press, pp. 175–191.

Hirschhorn, L. & Gilmore, T. (1990) The new boundaries of the "boundaryless" company. *Harvard Business Review*, **70,** 104–115.

Hughes, W. (1986) *Fleet Tactics: Theory and Practice.* Annapolis, MD: Naval Institute Press.

Koch, B. A. (1993) Differentiating reliability seeking organizations from other organizations: Development and validation of an assessment device. In K. H. Roberts (Ed.) *New Challenges to Understanding Organizations.* New York: Macmillan, pp. 75–97.

Kovach, K. A. & Render, B. (1987) NASA managers and Challenger: A profile and possible explanation. *Personnel*, **64,** 40–44.

Miles, R. E. & Snow, C. C. (1986) Organizations: New concepts for new forms. *California Management Review*, **28,** 62–73.

Mitroff, I. & Mohrman, S. (1986) The whole system is broke and in desperate need of fixing: Notes on the second industrial revolution. *International Journal of Technology Management*, **1,** 65–75.

Moorhead, G., Ference, R. J. & Neck, C. (1991) Group decision fiascoes continue: Space shuttle Challenger and a revised group think framework. *Human Relations*, **44,** 539–550.

Nelson, R. E. (1991) Network characteristics of high performing organizations. *Journal of Business Communication*, **28,** 367–386.

Perrow, C. (1979) *Complex Organizations: A Critical Essay*, Second edition. New York: Random House.

Perrow, C. (1984) *Normal Accidents.* New York: Basic Books.

Perrow, C. (1986) *Complex Organizations: A Critical Essay*, Third edition. New York: Random House.

Read, P. P. (1993) *Ablaze: The Story of the Heroes and Victims of Chernobyl*. New York: Random House.

Roberts, K. H. (1990) Some characteristics of high reliability organizations. *Organization Science*, **1**, 160–177.

Roberts, K. H. & Moore, W. H. (1993) Bligh Reef dead ahead: The grounding of the Exxon-Valdez. In K. H. Roberts (Ed.) *New Challenges to Organizations*. New York: Macmillan, pp.231–247.

Roberts, K. H., Rousseau, D. M. & La Porte, T. R. (in press) The culture of high reliability: Quantitative and qualitative assessment abroad nuclear powered aircraft carriers. *Journal of High Technology Management Research*.

Roberts, K. H., Stout, S. & Halpern, J. J. (in press) Decision dynamics in two high reliability military organizations. *Management Science*.

Schulman, P. (1993) The analysis of high reliability organizations: A comparative framework. In K. H. Roberts (Ed.) *New Challenges to Understanding Organizations*. New York: Macmillan, pp.33–53.

Schwartz, H. S. (1987) On the psychodynamics of organizational disaster: The case of the space shuttle Challenger. *Columbia Journal of World Business*, **22**, 59–67.

Senge, P. (1990) *The Fifth Discipline: The Art and Practice of the Learning Organization*. New York: Doubleday/Currency.

Shrader, C. B., Lincoln, J. R. & Hoffman, A. V. (1989) The network structure of organizations: Effects of task contingencies and distributional form. *Human Relations*, **42**, 43–66.

Shrivastava, P. (1987) *Bhopal: Anatomy of a Crisis*. Cambridge, MA: Ballinger.

Starbuck, W. H. & Milliken, F. J. (1988) Challenger: Fine tuning the odds until something breaks. *Journal of Management Studies*, **25**, 319–340.

US Department of the Navy. Office, Chief of Naval Operations. *Composite Warfare Commanders Manual*, NWP-10.

Vaughan, D. (1990) Autonomy, interdependence and social control: NASA and the space shuttle challenger. *Administrative Science Quarterly*, **35**, 225–257.

Warren, R., Rose, S. & Bergunder, A. (1974) *The Structure of Urban Reform*. Lexington, Mass.: Lexington Books.

Weick, K. E. (1987) Organizational culture as a source of high reliability. *California Management Review*, **29**, 112–127.

Weick, K. E. (1990) The vulnerable system: An analysis of the Tenerife air disaster. *Journal of Management*, **16**, 571–593.

Weick, K. E. & Roberts, K. H. (1993) Collective mind in organizations: Heedful interrelating on flight decks. *Administrative Science Quarterly*, **38**, 357–381.

Wheatley, M. (1992) *Leadership and the New Science*. San Francisco, Ca: Berrett-Koehler.

Wholey, D. & Hounker, J. W. (1993) Effects of generalized and niche overlap on network linkages among youth service agencies. *Academy of Management Journal*, **36**, 349–371.

Wise, C. R. (1989) Whither federal organizations: The air safety challenge and federal management's response. *Public Administration Review*, **49**, 17–28.

CHAPTER 2

Meso Organizational Behavior: Avoiding Three Fundamental Biases[1]

Denise M. Rousseau
Northwestern University, Evanston, USA

and

Robert J. House
University of Pennsylvania, Philadelphia, USA

"Is she micro or macro?" In the field of organizational behavior (OB), this is a professional issue rather than a personal question. A common inquiry in situations ranging from faculty recruiting to informal conversations, this question reflects the typical alignment that organizational scholars assign each other based on two prevailing research perspectives. The micro perspective is associated with psychological phenomena. The macro one is linked to socioeconomic features of organizations. However, a trend in organizational research may make the opening question both unanswerable and outmoded—the emergence of meso organizational research as a third paradigm, one that

---

[1] Many arguments posed in this chapter are based on "If it ain't Meso, it ain't OB" (House & Rousseau, 1991), a position paper written for the Meso Organization Studies Team, and "The third paradigm: meso organizational research comes of age", written with Melissa Thomas (House, Rousseau & Thomas, 1993). Thanks are due to Dan Levin for helpful comments.

Trends in Organizational Behavior, Volume 1. Edited by C. L. Cooper and D. M. Rousseau
© 1994 John Wiley & Sons Ltd.

is both more integrative and more *organizational* (House & Rousseau, 1992; House, Rousseau & Thomas, in press). It identifies three fundamental biases non-meso research risks and the role the Meso perspective can play in the field's future.

WHAT IS MESO?

The term meso implies "in between" as in mezzanine or mezzo, or mesomorph (House & Rousseau, 1992). Meso used in the context of research refers to an integration of micro and macro theory in the study of processes specific to organizations which by their very nature are a synthesis of psychological and socioeconomic processes. Meso research occurs in an organizational context where processes at two or more levels are investigated simultaneously. Its thesis is that micro and macro processes cannot simply be treated separately and then added up to understand organizations (House, Rousseau & Thomas, in press). Many concepts of special interest to organizational researchers cannot be understood by studying one level by itself: they span or entrain several units or levels at the same time. Concepts such as leadership, networking, power or control can bridge people, units, or levels. Other phenomena occur only in organizations such as *organizational* learning (Huber, 1991), citizenship (Organ, 1990), or climate (Schneider, 1990).

OB has long been divided into research focusing on individual-level experiences (e.g. attitudes and motivation) and those focusing on organizational level outcomes (e.g. strategic change, structure–environment contingencies). From the perspective of micro-oriented OB research, the focus has largely been on individual perceptions, experiences and values. Classic micro-OB research focuses on individual attitudes, cognitions, performance, and behaviors. Research on commitment, typical of the micro perspective, largely addresses individual perceptions and experiences (Mathieu & Zajac, 1990; Rousseau & Wade-Benzoni, in press), providing abundant evidence of the role that individual factors play in shaping a person's attachment to an employer. However, the role of organizational factors in commitment has largely been overlooked since commitment research focuses on studies within a single organization (see Mathieu and Zajac, 1990 for a review of the commitment literature). Studying commitment in a single organization leads researchers to overlook the causal underpinnings from situational factors and overestimates the role played by individual-level variables. Neglect of organizational causes of member responses is troubling given the evidence that commitment may in fact not be a specific individual response at all but a "two way street" based upon the quality of the interaction between employee and employer (e.g. Eisenberger et al, 1986; Shore & Wayne, in press; Rousseau & Wade-Benzoni, in press). But unless studies of individuals are conducted in several organizations at the same time, it is impossible for micro researchers to identify contributions made by organizational factors.

From a macro point of view, there are glaring omissions as well. A number of major theories generalize from organizations to individuals and back again without addressing the psychological characteristics of the individuals involved (House & Rousseau, 1991). Theories addressing agency (Alchian & Demsetz, 1972), resource dependence (Pfeffer & Salancik, 1978) and transaction costs (Williamson, 1979) assume individuals are self-serving and opportunistic. Empirical studies employing these frameworks carry forward these untested assumptions. Agency theory takes a stylized view of stockholder–CEO and organization–employee relations. By reducing relationships to principal-agent contracts, the impact of personal relationships, levels of involvement, and units of analysis (person or firm) is summarily dismissed. A test of principal and agent behavior offering no description of either party is a limited test. Resource dependency theory assumes all individuals acquire and exercise power when structural characteristics of their position allow them to do so. However, Enz (1988) demonstrates that personal characteristics make a difference in position power. She observes that the amount of power individuals enjoy depends also on congruence between personal values and those of the organization's dominant coalition. Similarly, transaction cost theory assumes opportunistic behavior (i.e. "self-interest seeking with guile", Williamson, 1979) regardless of personal values or levels of moral development. Assuming away individual differences and context (including the quality of the relationships involved) severely limits the applicability of macro models in explaining the behavior of top management team members let alone the responses of the larger organization.

To overcome these limits we have proposed meso as a third, more integrative paradigm for the field of organizational behavior (House & Rousseau, 1991; House, Rousseau & Thomas, in press). A meso framework involves simultaneous consideration of main and interaction effects at several levels. Moreover, by moving beyond the narrow confines of a single unit of analysis, a meso framework encourages questions about the meaning of levels and units of study to the understanding of organizational behavior. Meso is both an integration of micro and macro OB and an emergence of OB *beyond micro/macro the constraints*. Key features considered in a meso approach to organizational behavior include:

- The effects of context on individual and group behavior.
- The construction of context by individual psychological processes and social dynamics.
- Parallels and discontinuities in behavioral processes across individuals, groups and organizations.
- Expansion of units of study to include abstract organizational features (e.g. routines and procedures) as well as activities (events and cycles).

Moving beyond micro/macro constraints takes the field forward in three ways:

- It creates more realistic theory and research.
- It expands the "units" of study beyond the deceptive tidiness of individual, group, and organization.
- It emphasizes the distinctive nature of behavioral processes *in and of organizations* (in contrast to generic individual behavior or stylized models of markets).

More realistic theory and research arises by questioning the use of micro and macro as boundaries. These two subdisciplines are not necessarily inherently a part of the phenomena we study. Each certainly reflects ways in which scholars have ordered their own professional world to give meaning to such concepts as "careers" or "programmatic research". But there is no necessary restriction of important causal variables to any particular level. Of course, all studies omit variables. Constraints on resources and our own cognitive limits make omission necessary. But systematic omission, without announcing the resulting limitations of such research, is bias.

Expanding the units of study in organizational behavior makes it possible to investigate behavior in organizations in terms not only of persons and organizations but also of events, routines, activities, and crises. The boundaries of micro and macro manifest themselves not only as biased selections of variables, but also in restricting units of study to the traditional focus of psychology, sociology and economics, namely, individuals, groups, and organizations. But are individuals, groups, and organizations the critical distinctive manifestations of "organizational behavior"? Karl Weick (1992) raises the question of whether we have reified certain structures in order to justify some preferred courses of action. Reified means to take an abstraction and convert it into a concrete thing. Living cells, organs, and individuals are concrete biological entities. Groups, organizations, and markets are not. Scientists use varying labels for comparable phenomena. For instance, what sociologists would term a "role system", OB researchers would label an "organization" (Simon, 1957). The latter term has the appearance of concreteness, but organizations are nonetheless collections of interdependent roles. The false concreteness of terms like group and organization makes them seem more like living entities in the fashion of cells, organs, and persons. In other cultures such as Japan or Uganda, it is often difficult to know where an organization ends and the larger social environment begins, so blurred are the boundaries between group and organizations and one organization and another. The emergence of networked organizations (Snow, Miles & Coleman, 1992) in the US may mean that organizations look (once again) more like role systems than concrete entities.

In complex organizations where many activities involve multiple units, it is often difficult to find an appropriate organizational level (e.g. division, department, work group) at which to study them. For multi-unit activities involving complex organizational processes, it may be better to focus not on traditional organizational units but rather on the *activities* which link these units. Routines (how customer complaints are handled) and events (the disasters associated with Bhopal, Three Mile Island, or the space shuttle Challenger) may make better units of study than organizations or persons for some critical organizational processes such as learning, change, or technology (e.g. Rousseau & Cooke, 1984). Routines such as standardized recipes and procedures are both abstractions, that is, models of how activities should be carried out to accomplish a task. In effect, routines are a dimension of the organization's technology perpetuating organizational know-how. Events can include ongoing activities (e.g. rule-following), observed behaviors (e.g. unsafe acts) or results (e.g. accidents). The same routines and events can be studied from the perspective of several levels even if a particular routine or event means different things to the organization than it does to its members. Safety procedures embody knowledge from the organization's perspective and can require compliance from the individual's. Disasters might help an organization to learn to do things better but might cause injury or death to an individual worker. The study of accidents is a study neither of individuals nor of organizations but the simultaneous study of both and more. Routines and events span the traditional individual–group–organization levels of analysis in organizational research; in fact, they may provide a shared focus of analysis across several disciplines (Weick, 1982; p. 180) from population ecology to group process. A shift from traditional organizational units to organizational activities creates the need to integrate micro and macro processes in the study of organizations.

Meso, the integration of micro and macro perspectives on organizations, is also critical to understanding essential *organizational* problems. This is so because routines and activities linking members to each other and larger organizational units are the very essence of organizations. Activities, such as work cycles and decision-making, and routines, such as performance programs and procedures, help us flesh out what organizations are. Units of study can be something other than hierarchical levels. Units also can include events, work cycles, decisions, accidents, crises, and routines. From philosopher/scholars such as Barnard (1938), organizational research has sought to understand what the basic organizational elements are that can produce cooperation and productivity. Barnard himself was reluctant to define or place boundaries around the "formal organization". Were Barnard alive today he might very possibly agree that organizations are more than hierarchies. Too, he might note that sometimes modern organizations are not even particularly formal or hierarchical. But even in the most bureaucratic, centralized firm, we can study all the levels in an organization from individual, to work group, to supervisors, and every level of management and still leave out some essential features of the organization. A meso perspective acknowledges that unit of study and organizational level can mean something different.

FUNDAMENTAL BIASES OF NON-MESO WORK

Having argued that OB must go beyond the confines of micro and macro approaches, we now describe what can occur when a meso approach is not adopted. There are three fundamental biases in non-meso work. Non-meso research runs the risk of:

- Overgeneralization—assuming parallels or isomorphisms in seemingly similar concepts across levels (e.g. learning, change).
- Underestimation of cross-level effects—studies of persons underestimate the effect of groups and organizations on individual behavior while studies of organizational settings underestimate the effects individuals have on their environments.
- Reification of organizational structures—key phenomena in organizations may not be tangible organizations and groups but other entities such as routines and events that motivate member responses.

Overgeneralization

Individuals and organizations have some activities in common. Each is said to make decisions, learn, set goals, perform and change. The same can be said of groups, subunits, departments and divisions. (Soon we will probably be extending these concepts to networks, dyads, and infrastructures.) Yet, it is unclear whether organizations and persons decide, learn, create goals, perform, and change in comparable ways. At issue here is whether such constructs as decision-making, learning, goal setting, performance and change are isomorphic. Isomorphic means that the underlying structure of a construct is the same across levels. To test for isomorphism we need to model the factors that give rise to each construct. Thus, if goal setting for individuals is a function of expectancies for success and instrumentalities for goal achievement, we would need evidence of comparable processes for groups and organizations to generalize findings from one level to another. The relative success of individual goal setting as a motivation tool and the large scale frustration often encountered in implementing organizational goal setting (e.g. corporate experiences with "management by objectives"; Ford, 1979) suggest that goal setting means different things at different levels.

Do the same processes apply across levels? Consider the case of organizational learning. Organizational learning has been defined as the acquisition of new behaviors (Huber, 1991; Goodman, 1993, personal communication). Like individual learning, it requires memory, the retention and retrieval of information. But organizational learning has two features that distinguish it from individual learning, communication and shared interpretation. Unless changes in behavior are communicated among members, organizational learning does not occur. Developing an electronic library that few people use does not constitute organizational learning. A service manager who discovers a new way to increase machine reliability but tells no one else manifests individual learning but not organizational. The memory or retention system for organizational learning is most effective when it stores information that is conducive to ready and wide access (e.g. procedures, newsletters, and electronic networks). Shared interpretations through interaction, feedback and integration of learning into ongoing activities promote both dissemination as well as the organization's assimilation of new behaviors. Interpretative processes in organizations are something more than what occurs within individuals (Daft & Weick, 1984). People come and go but organizations preserve knowledge, mental maps, norms and values creating a thread of coherence in what characterizes organizational interpretations. Weick (1992) has argued that routines are the core of organizations. Routines can be vital to organizational memory. Regular meetings of in-house experts promote shared learning as do ongoing practices of benchmarking, analysis, and follow-up. Individual learning is not necessarily social, but organizational learning is inherently interactive, interpretative and integrative. If organizational and individual learning are unalike in basic respects, it is plausible that other seemingly comparable multilevel concepts are too.

We suspect the assumption of isomorphism is overused in organizational research. How likely is isomorphism between individual and organizational growth, between individual and group decision-making, between organizational performance and individual success at tasks? Yet frequently, the descriptions of one evoke constructions from the other. Isomorphisms offer tremendous power and scope in identifying broad patterns in individual, group, and organizational processes. J. G. Miller's (1978) *Living Systems* perhaps best illustrates the scope of basic multi-level processes, finding parallels at every level from the cell to the supranational state. People can overassume parallels, however. We wonder whether the ambiguities and uncertainty in complex organizational processes have made it difficult for researchers to conceptualize the separate processes of people and of organizations as distinct.

There is a good deal of evidence in other disciplines that divergent processes can operate at different levels. Research on such distinct entities as ants and Frenchmen observes differences across levels. Considered the behavior of army ants. A group of three ants can carry an item that is so large that these ants could not individually carry the fragments of the item even if they broke it into three pieces (Frank, 1989). How is the superefficiency of teams achieved? The ant team achieves superefficiency by balancing the large item in such a way that rotational forces—which an individual would have to strain against—disappear. In addition, by timing their leg movements so that members are out of step, a team can keep more load bearing legs on the ground, per capita, per unit of time, than can an individual. Clearly the collective capacity of army ants is a whole greater than the sum of its parts. Routines, such as patterns of walking in step, have different effects when a load is shared or a load is individually carried.

Now consider the interesting case of the French, French politics, and American attitudes toward them both. Allison and Messick (1985) describe reactions to the 1986 American attack on Libya for its involvement in international terrorism. More than two dozen US warplanes took off from Lakenheath air base in England. The most direct flight path involved crossing French airspace. But French president François Mitterrand refused to allow the US to fly over France. As a result the planes were forced to circumvent the Iberian peninsula, doubling the length of their flight to Libya. Following the raid in which two American pilots were lost. Americans were heard complaining about the lack of French support while praising British loyalty. But, a

Newsweek magazine poll, conducted shortly after the raid revealed that only 30% of the British but 61% of the French approved of the raid.

The noncorrespondence between French (and British) actions and their attitudes and US perceptions indicates that collectives, averages, and individuals can reflect distinct attitudes and behaviors. The whole in the case is different from the sum of its parts. Allison and Messick (1985) coined the concept "group attribution error" to characterize people's tendency to assume a direct correspondence between a group choice and the preferences or attitudes of the group's members. We raise the question of whether the tendency of researchers to assume parallels across levels is part of the same tendency to overgeneralize from one level to another. Kahneman and Tversky (1972) proposed a general cognitive bias (in their terms a "heuristic") where people are willing to make generalizations to a population based on a single sample regardless of its typicality or representativeness. Just as collectives can have different properties from the average individual within the group, so too might organizational preferences, choices, and evaluations be distinct from the units or members within it. Yet, people tend to believe that an organization's decision is representative of its members' attitudes even when available information suggests otherwise. Following from Allison and Messick (1985), we must consider whether there is a phenomenon here that might be the "fundamental organizational attribution error". The individual-level counterpart of the organizational attribution bias is anthropomorphizing, that is, assigning personal traits to groups and organizations (Roberts, Hulin & Rousseau, 1978; Rousseau, 1985). Many presumed isomorphisms in OB may essentially reflect attribution bias.

Overgeneralization also takes the form of failure to recognize discontinuities across levels. Consider the phenomenon of the performance paradox. The performance paradox refers to the observation in a wide variety of organizational studies that organization performance measures are unrelated *at the same level* as well as *across levels* (Rousseau, 1992). Indicators of overall organizational performance are notoriously low in their correlations with each other (e.g. Seashore, Indik & Georgopoulos, 1960). Organizations good on one indicator (efficiency or cost) are not necessarily good at others (e.g. quality, customer satisfaction). This weak link in performance *at the same level* is compounded by noncorrespondence between performance of organizations and their subunits. Tremendous investments may be made which improve the efficiency of a department or the skills of a work group and yet the overall organization does not improve. Goodman, Lerch & Mukhopadhyay (1992) attribute this asymmetry to the organization's failure to manage linkages across levels. The capacity of a high performing work unit to positively impact the overall organization is tied to the organization's response to that unit's high performance. If the practices behind the unit's improved quality or efficiency are disseminated to other units, the entire organization may see performance gains. If on the other hand, local gains are not disseminated or if that extra high level of performance is not integrated in to the organization's workflow (e.g. it might be turned instead into "slack" resources, where the extra goods produced are warehoused until needed), we can have a highly performing work unit in a mediocre organization. This performance paradox comes about because although organizational performance is tied to subunit success, how this interdependence is managed affects the ability of the part to benefit the whole.

Ants, the French, and the performance paradox provide evidence of discontinuities across level. From a meso perspective, the discontinuities each manifests suggests organizational scholars should be mindful of:

- The tendency toward attribution errors (i.e. fundamental organizational attribution errors and anthropomorphizing) in generalizing from persons to organizations and back again.
- The need to test for isomorphism rather than assume it.

Underestimating Cross-level Effects

Single-level research cannot help but overestimate local effects and underestimate cross-level ones. A focus on individual factors in studying a person's behavior or organizational characteristics in investigating organizational outcomes belies a contemporary truth: organizations and their members are highly interdependent. Tom Peters (1991) characterized industry trends toward increased competition, delayering, and extensive designer–producer–customer relations in terms of a "declaration of interdependence". This trend applies to organizational scholarship as well. Once upon a time, in the classic hierarchical organization, scholars came to view effects at one level as large isolated from those at another. Several decades ago, Herbert Simon (1973) argued that parts of organizations were nearly decomposable, that is, organizational processes and levels were very segmented. This means that researchers could study one level or one department without considering another. To make this point, Simon relayed the classic fable of the watchmaker:

> Two watchmakers assemble fine watches, each watch containing ten thousand parts. Each watchmaker is interrupted frequently to answer the phone. The first has organized his total assembly operation into a sequence of subassemblies; each subassembly is a stable arrangement of 100

elements, each watch a stable arrangement of 100 subassemblies. The second watch maker has developed no such organization. The average interval between phone interruptions is a time long enough to assemble about 150 elements. An interruption causes any set of elements that does not yet form a stable system to fall apart completely. By the time he has answered about eleven phone calls, the first watchmaker will usually have finished assembling a watch. The second watchmaker will almost never succeed in assembling one—he will suffer the fate of Sisyphus: as often as he rolls the rock up the hill, it will roll down again. (Simon, 1973; pp. 7–8.)

The moral of the story suggests that there is an adaptive advantage to hierarchies, elements of subsystems retain their organization when other subsystems are under stress or suffer setbacks. If subassemblies and levels in hierarchies are intended to make the parts nearly decomposable and easily studied separately, all subassemblies must function separately from all others. People cannot rotate between units, serve more than one boss, or sit on committees in more than one department. If this was once true, it is almost certainly less than true today.

Top/down and Bottom/up Effects

The neat image of a hierarchy built on self-contained parts ignores two behavioral features. First, people have a hand in constructing the organization in which they are members. Higher level units are not easily separated from their component parts. Individuals shape their work groups, departments, networks, and larger organization. Individual predilections can become organizational norms. In organizations, people who share a belief that team work is desirable can become the basis of a team-oriented culture. For this reason, organizations seeking to change their norms often bring in new members with different beliefs (Schneider, 1987). Lower level processes create higher ones through mechanisms such as social construction, ongoing interaction patterns, and shared values. The more unstructured, novel, or ambiguous the situation, the more influence lower level processes will have.

The second behavioral feature is that in complex organizations, individuals are embedded in larger units, and organizations are parts of larger systems (Roberts, this volume). Higher level processes can direct, control, and reward lower level ones. Settings do shape people. Although we know that personality affects how individuals behave under conditions of ambiguity (e.g. crises, novel settings), situational factors are powerful determinants of behavior in the majority of settings (Mischel, 1973). The watchmaker fable reflects a time when loose coupling was seen as a source of flexibility (Weick, 1976). Today it often appears more as slack and inefficiency. Loose linkages between parts were suited to an era of low competition and long product life cycles.

To quote Victor Hugo, "There is one thing stronger than all the armies in the world, and that is an idea whose time has come". Part of the debureaucratization of contemporary organizations has been the cutting of managerial layers and the elimination of slack. One might also argue that near decomposability is going by the wayside, also. A meso approach to research can readily accommodate the likelihood that what hierarchy remains in modern organizations will have less slack and little buffering. Thus, one level's potential effect on another is very likely much greater in many contemporary firms than in a traditional, bureaucratic environment. However, whereas cross-level effects previously emphasized control-oriented processes (e.g. organizational rewards for individual or group behavior) increasingly the inter-level effects involve more *relational* issues. Graen and Scandura (1987) find ample evidence for mutual and dyadic influences between managers and their subordinates. Emphasizing the nature of the exchange, trust and other indicators of relationship quality, they observe that the relationship is less between level but more between persons (where one might be a hierarchical superior or team leader). Ancona (1990) observes that how work groups manage their relations with their bosses may be more important to their performance than the way the work group manages itself.

Similarly, contemporary and future effects between levels may take on less of a control quality and more of a coordinating or synergistic quality as interdependence between levels must be managed to improve productivity (Goodman et al, 1993). Ancona and Chong (1991) have adopted the biological concept of entrainment to describe how processes at one level adjust to those at another. Entrainment is the adjustment of one behavior to be in rhythm with another. Entrainment is evident in chief executive officer (CEO) succession where CEO changes accompany changes in the top management team. When changes in CEO are entrained to those in the top management team, overall firm performance improves (Virany, Tuschman & Romanelli, 1992). If this entrainment fails to occur, the firm has a tougher time responding to environmental changes. Similarly, the performance paradox arises when the organization in general is unable to respond in kind to productivity gains made in a department or division due to inertia, poor communication, or failing to learn and adopt the innovations developed by the department or division.

Interactive Effects

Not all cross-level effects are top/down or bottom/up. Some are interactive, involving mutual and simultaneous effects at several levels. McCain, O'Reilly and Pfeffer (1983) have shown that being older in a group dominated by younger members leads to increased older member propensity to leave. Effects are both group level (heterogeneity/turnover rate) and individual (similarity/desire to leave). Interactive effects are observed in research on organizational commitment and citizenship as well. Both are linked to individual attributes as well as to the quality of the relationship between individual and organization, and the support the organization provides its members. Commitment and citizenship are context-specific behaviors (meaning the same people may show different behaviors depending on the setting) and, therefore, require simultaneous consideration of features at several levels.

Top/down, bottom/up and interactive effects make it difficult to meaningfully study behavior in complex organizations at any single level. Traditional single-level research may be the moral equivalent of looking for the lost wallet under the street lamp because it is easier to see (not because it is likely to be there).

Reified Organizational Structures

The real key entities in OB may not be the traditional individual/group/organization units we frequently describe. Traditional units of study may be reified structures, that is, presumed entities created in order to justify preferred styles of research. Work on networked organizations and externalized offices points to the arbitrariness of our notions of organization (Kanter, 1989; Venkatesh & Vitalari, 1992). The rise of "hollow corporations" outsourcing technical as well as support functions (*Business Week*, 1986) suggests that individuals, groups, and organizations may be less relevant to the study of some organizations than are routines and activities employed to achieve the organization's task and to manage its relationships. How would we study performance, change, and decision-making in an organization with no ongoing employees? What if an organization's primary workers are employed by, and identify with, some other firm? We suspect that at this juncture organizational research is itself undergoing a major transition. A dimension of this change is the shift in units of study. In a review of research published from 1987 to 1993, the fastest growing domain among those studies identified as meso focused upon networks, routines, or relationships (House et al, in press). There is tremendous expansion in research into units of study beyond traditional levels of analysis (i.e. individuals, groups, and organizations).

Two emergent trends are behind the movement to question whether hierarchies and levels are primary or even appropriate units of study in organizational research. One is a critique of positivism that flourishes in many forms (e.g. postmodernism and social constructionism), but is exemplified in feminist approaches to organizational research. Another is the evolution among contemporary organizations toward forms which are networked, delayered, communal, integrated or otherwise unlike the hierarchical bureaucracy of traditional Western organizations.

Contrasting what they refer to as mainstream or positivistic approaches, McGrath, Kelly and Rhodes (in press) offer what they term a feminist critique of organizational research. They argue that traditional OB research treats subjects out of context (e.g. studies groups but ignores the work they do, looks at individual values but not the organization they have joined) and views the world as having one concrete, unified reality all subject to the same (physical) laws. In contrast they say, organizations, like many other societal creations, may reflect multiple realities depending on the vantage point of observer and subjects. Rather than decontextualizing the subject, a feminist view emphasizes relationships. Potentially, then, all behavior is a function of both person and the setting in which that person interacts. Rather than identifying a person as extroverted or introverted, the observer might discover that the person is introverted on the job and with strangers but extroverted with friends and family. This view of self as interdependent with setting is consistent with non-Western views of personality (Markus & Kitayama, 1991), highlighting the cultural myopia that operates not only in organizational research but in personality theory and social-cognition as well. One relationship of critical import from a feminist perspective is that of scientist and subject. A feminist perspective suggests that researcher values operate in problem selection, in the use of "key informant" data as more objective than employee self reports. All research can be viewed as a process of interpretation, with no such thing as value-free objective observation. To focus attention on hierarchy or managers is value-laden regardless of the validity of the research instrument and methodology. Weick (1992) observes:

> There is an intensifying search for alternatives to hierarchy as a means to coordinate action . . . and some of the most interesting suggestions are coming from feminists . . . . Using the feminist discussions, for example, the most dramatic reading of the literature on high-reliability organizations could be captured in the phrase, "patriarchy kills people". The organizational forms found in . . . nuclear plants and in aircrews . . . resemble closely the military organizational form (p. 180).

Alternatives to hierarchy can mean viewing organizations as networks or social constructions, opening up organizational research to alternative organizational models that are neither micro nor macro.

New organizational forms do not fit neatly into old boundaries.

Centralized hierarchies are being displaced by clusters of business units coordinated by market mechanisms, by interactions among numerous designers, producers and distributors (Snow, Miles & Coleman, 1992). Network partners need not be members of the same organization, may each be separate legal entities, or may reflect several distinct organizational forms. Organizational research has had difficulties extending its models to non-hierarchical as well as non-Western settings (often because non-hierarchical is non-Western or at least non-US). A commentator once observed "Japan is Sociology's revenge on Economics". But in a larger sense, the blurry boundaries of networks and escalating interdependence of modern organizations challenge the fundamental, self-contained views of organizations and individuals that micro and macro approaches perpetuate.

Combining insights from alternative research perspectives with concerns of emerging organizational forms, a meso approach affords:

- Investigation of fundamental building blocks of organizations including elements which are concrete, abstract and activity-based.
- Richer and more diverse interpretations of the meaning and functioning of organizations and actions within and by them.
- Deeper understanding of our assumptions as researchers and the role we play in shaping organizations of the future.

CONCLUSION

Organizational research discovered systems theory in the 1960s (e.g. Katz & Kahn, 1966) and with it Ashby's law (Ashby, 1952). The principle it espoused, "only variety destroys variety", argues that flexibility is more advantageous in a dynamic environment than in a static one. Applied to research, Ashby's law suggests that we need problem solvers as complex as the problems we face. Certainly we need models that are as rich as the phenomena they would portray. The micro and macro distinction is an oversimplification, suited to an era where organizations were assumed to be relatively static and persons relatively homogeneous. The three biases of non-meso work reflect the reality and the cognitive limits of the field in an earlier era.

All research omits variables. This is necessary and often efficient. But unannounced and systematic omission is bias. Information systems and a more sophisticated field have made complexity more tolerable. To pursue the study of organizations more fully, we may not need new concepts, but we do need to use the ones we have better and more integratively.

REFERENCES

Alchian, A. A. & Demsetz, H. (1972) Production, information cause, and economic organization. *American Economic Review*, **62**, 777–795.

Allison, S. T. & Messick, D. M. (1985) The group attribution error. *Journal of Experimental Social Psychology*, **21**, 563–579.

Allison, S. T. & Messick, D. M. (1987) From individual inputs to group outputs, and back again. Group processes and inferences about members. In C. Hendricks (Ed.) *Review of Personality and Social Psychology*, **8**, 111–143.

Ancona, D. (1990) Outward bound: Strategies for team survival in an organization. *Academy of Management Journal*, **33**, 334–364.

Ancona, D. & Chong, D. C. (1991) Entrainment: Cycles of synergy in organizational behavior. Sloan School of Management. Massachusetts Institute of Technology, Cambridge.

Ashby, W. R. (1952) *Design for a Brain*. New York: Wiley.

Barnard, C. I. (1938) *The Functions of the Executive*. Cambridge, MA: Harvard University Press.

Business Week (1986) The hollow corporation. 3 March.

Daft, R. L. & Weick, K. (1984) Toward a model of organizations as interpretative systems. *Academy of Management Review*, **9**, 284–295.

Eisenberger, R., Huntington, R., Hutchinson, S. & Sowa, D. (1986) Perceived organizational support. *Journal of Applied Psychology*, **71**, 500–507.

Enz, C. (1988) The role of value congruity in intraorganizational power. *Administrative Science Quarterly*, **33**, 284–3-4.

Ford, C. H. (1979) MBO: An idea whose time has gone? *Business Horizons*, December, 49.

Frank, N. R. (1989) Army ants: A collective intelligence. *American Scientist*, March–April, 139–146.

Goodman, P. S., Lerch, J. & Mukhopadhyay, T. (1992) *Linkages and Performance Improvements*. Washington, DC: National Research Council.

Graen, G. B. & Scandura, T. A. (1987) Toward a psychology of dyadic organizing. In L. L. Cummings & B. M. Staw (Eds.) *Research in Organizational Behavior*, Vol. 9. Greenwich, CT: JAI Press, pp.175–208.

Heydebrand, W. (1989) New organizational forms. *Work and Occupations* **16**, 323–357.

House, R. J. & Rousseau, D. M. (1991) If it ain't Meso, it ain't OB. Position paper Meso Organization Studies Team. Wharton School of Business, University of Pennsylvania .

House, R., Rousseau, D. M. & Thomas, M. (1995) The third paradigm: Meso organizational research comes of age. In L. L. Cummings and B. M. Staw (Eds.) *Research in Organizational Behavior*, Vol. 17, in preparation.

Huber, G. P. (1991) Organizational learning: The contributing processes and literatures. *Organizational Science*, **2**, 88–115.

Hyde, C. (1989) A feminist model for macro-practice: Promises and problems. *Administration in Social Work*, **13**, 145–181.

Kahneman, D. & Tversky, A. (1972) Subjective probability: A judgement of representativeness. *Cognitive Psychology*, **3**, 430–454.

Kanter, R. M. (1989) *When Giants Learn to Dance*. New York: Simon and Schuster.

Katz, D. & Kahn, R. L. (1966) *The Social Psychology of Organizations*. New York: Wiley.

Markus, H. R. & Kitayama, S. (1991) Culture and self: Implications for cognition, emotion, and motivation. *Psychological Review*, **98**, 224–253.

Mathieu, J. E. & Zajac, D. M. (1990) A review and meta-analysis of the antecendents, correlates and consequences of organizational commitment. *Psychological Bulletin*, **108**, 171–194.

McCain, B. B., O'Reilly, C. A. & Pfeffer, J. (1983) The effects of departmental demography on turnover. *Academy of Management Journal*, **26**, 626–641.

McGrath, J. E., Kelly, J. R. & Rhodes, J. E. (in press) A feminist perspective on research methodology: Some metatheoretical issues, contrasts, and choices. In S. Oskamp & Costanzo, M. (Eds.) *Gender Issues in Social Psychology*. Sage Publications.

Miller, J. G. (1978) *Living Systems*. New York: McGraw-Hill.

Mischel, W. (1973) Toward a cogitive social learning reconceptualization of personality. *Psychological Review*, **80**, 252–283.

Organ, D. W. (1990) The motivational bases of organizational citizenship behavior. In B. M. Staw & L. L. Cummings (Eds.) *Research in Organizational Behavior*, Vol. 12. Greenwich, CT: JAI Press, pp. 43–72.

Peters, T. (1990) Declaration of interdependence. *San Jose Mercury*, July 4.

Pfeffer, J. & Salancik, G. R. (1978) *The External Control of Organization: A Resource Dependence Perspective*. New York: Harper and Row.

Roberts, K., Hulin, G. L. & Rousseau, D. M. (1978) *Developing an Interdisciplinary Science of Organization*. San Francisco: Jossey-Bass.

Rousseau, D. M. (1985) Issues of level in organizational research: Multi-level and cross-level perspectives. In L. L. Cummings & B. M. Staw (Eds.) *Research in Organizational Behavior*, Vol. 7. Greenwich, CT: JAI Press, pp. 1–37.

Rousseau, D. M. (1992) *Teamwork: Inside and Out*. Business Week/Advance Publications.

Rousseau, D. M. & Cooke, R. A. (1984) Technology and structure: The concrete, abstract, and activity systems of organizations. *Journal of Management*, **10**, 345–361.

Rousseau, D. M. & Wade-Benzoni, K. A. (in press) Changing individual–organization attachments: A two way street. In A. Howard (Ed.) *Changing Nature of Work*. Frontiers of Industrial and Organizational Psychology Series. San Francisco: Jossey-Bass.

Schneider, B. (1987) The people make the place. *Personnel Psychology*, **40**, 437–453.

Schneider, B. (1990) *Organizational Climate and Culture*. San Francisco: Jossey-Bass.

Seashore, S. E., Indik, B. P. & Georgopolous, B. S. (1960) Relationships among criteria of job performance. *Journal of Applied Psychology*, **44**, 195–202.

Shore, L. M. & Wayne, S. J. (in press) Commitment and employee behavior: A comparison of affective commitment and continuance commitment with perceived organizational support. *Journal of Applied Psychology*.

Simon, H. A. (1957) *Administrative Behavior*. New York: Free Press.

Simon, H. A. (1973) The organization of complex systems. In H. H. Pattee (Ed.), *Hierarchy Theory: The Challenge of Complex Systems*. New York: Braziller.

Snow, C. C., Miles, R. E. & Coleman, H. J. (1992) Managing 21st century network organizations. *Organizational Dynamics*, 5–21 (winter).

Venkatesh, A. & Vitalari, N. P. (1992) An emerging distributed work arrangement: An investigation of computer-based supplemental work at home. *Management Science*, **38**, 1687–1706.

Virany, B. B., Tuschman, M. & Romanelli, E. (1992) Executive succession and organizational outcomes in turbulent environments: An organizational learning approach. *Organizational Science*, **3**, 72–91.

Weick, K. E. (1976) Educational organizations as loosely coupled systems. *Administrative Science Quarterly*, **21**, 1–19.

Weick, K. E. (1992) Agenda setting in Organizational Behavior: A theory-focused approach. *Journal of Management Inquiry*, **1**, 171–183.

Williamson, O. (1979) Transaction-cost economics: The governance of contractual relations. *Journal of Law and Economics*, **3**, 233–261.

CHAPTER 3

Coordinating Global Companies: The Effects of Electronic Communication, Organizational Commitment, and a Multi-Cultural Managerial Workforce[1]

Maddy Janssens
Katholieke Universiteit Leuven, Belgium

and

Jeanne M. Brett
Northwestern University, Evanston, USA

Global companies face a strategic challenge to manage simultaneously local responsiveness, global integration, and innovation. In this paper we discuss three important factors that are impacting global organizations' ability to coordinate their activities: electronic voice and data networks,

---

[1] Organizations embedded in networks of suppliers, competitors, and customers also have significant inter-organizational coordination problems which are in many ways similar to the intra-organizational coordination problems discussed in this paper. However, inter-organizational networks provide fewer opportunities for coordination and control through human resources policies and practices and are not discussed here.

Trends in Organizational Behavior, Volume 1. Edited by C. L. Cooper and D. M. Rousseau
© 1994 John Wiley & Sons Ltd.

the abandonment of internal labor markets, and a truly multi-cultural managerial workforce. We analyze the impact these developments pose for the coordination of global companies and suggest research and policy initiatives to cope with them.

We begin with a vision of a global organization in the 1990s and a description of its coordination requirements for which several authors recommend coordination through socialization. We then consider the implications of electronic voice and data networks, the abandonment of internal labor markets, and the reality of a truly multi-cultural managerial workforce for coordination via socialization. We close with a discussion of alternative ways to coordinate and a set of research and policy initiatives.

ORGANIZING A GLOBAL COMPANY

Vision of a Global Company

Global companies, those with assets and resources widely dispersed geographically, are confronted with the strategic challenges to respond to local needs, to achieve global economies of scale, and to innovate one place in the world and transfer that learning elsewhere in the world (Bartlett & Ghoshal, 1989). To achieve these goals, coordination problems are enormous. Teams, not individuals, will be the basic organizational building blocks (Gerstein & Shaw, 1992; Snow, Miles & Coleman, 1992), and strategic decisions will be negotiated by groups whose members cross national, functional, and hierarchical boundaries.

The question addressed by this paper is how to achieve coordination within global organizations. The coordination issues we address are aspects such as group decision making, aligning individual and organizational interests, and the existence of conflicting perspectives. The research questions we raise and the practical advice we give focus on these three types of coordination problems.

Coordinating a Global Company

Historically, coordination in global companies has been by centralization (decision making by a cadre of top managers), formalization (decision making by reference to rules and procedures), socialization (decision making by reference to corporate norms and values) or some mix of the above strategies. Now, organizations are learning that the main aim of organizing is not to control stability and establish order, but to deal with instability and permanent change (Reed & Hughes, 1992). The teams, loosely-coupled systems, and networks that have also evolved in global companies seem to ask for new ways of coordinating.

Bartlett and Ghoshal (1989) advise that coordination can be achieved via a clear, shared understanding of company's objectives, reinforced by visible behavior and public action by top management and personnel policies that control managerial selection, career development, and training opportunities. Top management may rely on informal channels of communication for coordination and can control this informal network by carefully selecting managers for team assignments, controlling access to and agendas of international meetings, and providing opportunities for interpersonal contact via management training. Bartlett and Ghoshal's (1989) advice to rely on socialization for coordination in global companies is based on their research into the most effective coordination techniques in use by global companies in the mid 1980s. More recently, they have been more explicit that structures and systems complicate rather than facilitate coordination and advise a matrix in the mind of managers instead of a concrete matrix structure (Bartlett & Ghoshal, 1990).

Bartlett and Ghoshal (1989) are not alone in their advice to rely heavily on socialization as a coordination mechanism. Other commentators (Gerstein & Shaw, 1992; Nordström, 1993), writing more recently about the global organization linked by electronic systems, suggest that the informal organization—norms and values rather than rules (formalization in Bartlett and Ghoshal's terms) and supervision (centralization)—will furnish the cohesion necessary to provide direction and achieve coordination among autonomous teams. They argue that a strongly held culture and a network of individuals who use their leadership skills will be the principal means of control in the diffused organization.

We suspect that coordination based on socialization may be severely challenged by three factors. First, although electronic systems open up informal channels of communication between managers, they eliminate social context which is the carrier of norms and values. Second, corporations' reduced commitment to internal labor markets has reduced managers' commitment to the organization and its unique way of doing business. Third, the hiring of large numbers of local country managers also contributes to the diffusion rather than cohesion of norms and values.

LIMITATIONS TO COORDINATION VIA SOCIALIZATION

Electronic Systems

Electronic communications systems help people cross physical, social and psychological barriers (Kiesler & Sproull, 1992). Kiesler and Sproull have been at the forefront of the research on text-based electronic communication systems. They point out that although introduced for the purposes of efficiency, electronic communication systems generally have unanticipated secondary effects. Among those effects are likely to be social rearrangements, reassessments of what is important, and altered behavior-guiding norms.

Text, voice only, and all but the most sophisticated video reduce or eliminate social context cues. Social context cues are important factors in individuals' behavior. Without such cues, people feel distant and anonymous. They produce self-centered and unregulated behaviors, are less polite, and show less concern about being evaluated or with being liked (Kiesler & Sproull, 1992).

Social context cues also affect group processes. Meetings held electronically lack the non-verbal cues and backchannel discussion that enable speakers in a face-to-face group to tell how their arguments are being received, and to whom to direct further discussion. Groups meeting electronically have greater difficulties reaching agreement than those meeting face to face, probably because the process of discussion is different. In research by Weisband (1992) the process in face-to-face groups was that the second speaker agreed with the first and by the time the third person spoke, his/her stand equalled the final group choice. In electronic groups, the third speaker's position was as far from the group's ultimate choice as the first speaker's was. Electronic group members apparently offer opinions before considering the opinions of others.

Of course, lack of social context cues may also have benefits. Participation is typically more equal in electronic text groups (Kiesler & Sproull, 1992). Electronic text equalizes access and eliminates ordering of speakers. Thus, when status differences among group members do not reflect task relevant skills, an electronic text meeting may increase the quality of input into the group's task.

Unfortunately, there has been little research on decision quality in electronic versus face-to-face groups (Kiesler & Sproull, 1992). In a series of studies of prospect theory, face-to-face groups were shown to be more risk averse for gains and more risk seeking for losses than individuals. Electronic groups, however, were risk seeking in all circumstances, and their decisions were better predicted by the pre-discussion majority than by prospect theory. Kiesler and Sproull (1992) speculate that the increased riskiness was due to the reduction in the amount of social information exchanged in the electronic groups, compared to the face-to-face groups.

Kiesler and Sproull (1992) conclude that when group decisions require complex thinking or subtle multiparty negotiation, when problems are ill-defined or decisions need to be ratified symbolically, face-to-face decision making is probably best. Electronic systems may be used to augment face-to-face decision making, but on the basis of current research they do not provide an adequate substitute.

> There is definitely a need for face-to-face interaction especially in issues such as interpreting data, and understanding the links of the team to the different clients and different functional units. (Interview with M. Avau, 29 June 1993.)

Organizational Commitment

The socialization model of organizational commitment is based on managers' clear understanding of the corporations' objectives and their close personal relationship to it. Sonnenfeld and Peiperl (1988) call these types of organizations, clubs. To become a member, managers must pass through recruitment, development and acculturation hurdles. But, once a member, managers are given substantial discretion to make decisions in the best interest of the company. Members of organizational clubs should be highly committed to the organization in whose values and objectives they have been indoctrinated. Traditionally, clubs have in turn guaranteed career progression via the internal labor market and lifetime employment.

The policy of promoting people from within undoubtedly sets up a system of intense socialization. However, global competition is forcing organizations to increasingly pay attention to workforce flexibility and abandon total reliance on internal labor market. Strategies that increase workforce flexibility include the use of short-term, casual and temporary contracts and hiring and firing policies (that is reliance on the external labor market), as well as externalizing work through the use of sub-contractors (Blyton & Morris, 1992). Evidence from North America, Europe, and Australia confirms that organizations are increasingly adapting policies that maximize workforce flexibility (e.g. Baglioni & Crouch, 1990; OECD, 1989).

The wave of large corporate mergers in the 1980s was the first sign that US top management—which was never as caught up with the socialization model as their European and Japanese competitors—could no longer keep the implicit promise of lifetime employment. Many top management teams were unable to retain control of the companies which they directed. They were the first out of the door, followed shortly thereafter by the middle managers whose skills duplicated those already present in the acquiring company, or whose values were not "right" for the new culture envisioned by the acquirer. Managers on international assignments frequently had nothing to come home to, as acquirers realigned and merged international businesses.

These waves or restructuring have spread with the slumping worldwide economy to European and Japanese based companies. Early retirements are the norm in Europe, ostensibly to compensate for zero growth and the very large pool of unemployed youth. While European labor laws and Japanese traditions make it more difficult to terminate mid-career managers and tend to simulate functional flexibility more than in the US, even these companies are being forced by global competition to use forms of workforce flexibility and make reductions in managerial ranks. For example, since 1990, Daimler-Benz has laid off 27 000 people, Siemens 13 000, and Philips 40 000 (*The Economist*, 1993). Even in Japan, lifetime employment, one of the pillars of Japanese management, is being questioned. A recent survey showed that 86% of top management in the 100 largest Japanese companies, believed that lifetime employment would disappear (*Manichi Daily News*, 1993).

Advocates of workforce flexibility run the danger of overstating the value of adaptability and responsiveness to change, and thereby simultaneously understating the importance of stability and continuity within organizations (Blyton & Morris, 1992). Workforce flexibility is a defensive strategy, a primarily ad hoc, short-term and opportunistic response to fluctuations in demand. This type of flexibility is in contradiction with the pursuit of a high level of employee commitment.

In contrast, offensive or long-term flexibility strategies are characterized by proactive human resource strategies in which emphasis is placed more on achieving an adaptable rather than a low-cost labor force. Functional flexibility, particularly where this entails investment in training employees to undertake a broader range and level of tasks, is central to the strategy of long-term flexibility (Blyton & Morris, 1992). Walton (1985) already argued that job security—although not absolute— is a higher priority for a commitment strategy than a control strategy. According to this author, the challenge is to give employees some assurance of security, perhaps by offering them priority in training and retaining as old jobs are eliminated.

> People leave the company because they are not satisfied, not because you invest in them. I believe that process-oriented training increases commitment more than business-oriented training. It gives a manager the signal that the organization believes in his/her career development. (Interview with M. Avau, 29 June 1993.)

The theoretical reflections that employee commitment will potentially be undermined by the introduction of different forms of flexible work and employment patterns, have found empirical evidence. According to

Hirsch (1987), the uncertainty and stress of restructuring took a toll on organizational commitment. Hirsch urged managers to exert control over their careers, to "pack their own parachutes" and become career free agents. US managers learned quickly. Reilly, Brett and Stroh (1993) collected data on managers' attitudes and corporate turbulence in 1989. One of the most consistent findings in their study was a strong relationship between corporate turbulence and career loyalty. Managers, seeing that their corporations could no longer promise lifetime employment and were no longer committed to the internal labor market, began to focus on managing their own careers, making themselves viable on the external labor market. Those who had been members of organizational clubs, with their company specific skills, found themselves least attractive on the external labor market.

Multi-Cultural Managerial Workforce

Several converging factors have caused global companies to shift from expatriate and third country staffing to staffing with local nationals. Two strategic factors have contributed to this shift. First, global companies have become increasingly aware of the need for local knowledge in order to be competitive. Second, global companies have come to realize that multi-national, multi-functional teams, rather than expatriate managers, can better handle decisions that balance local needs and global economies of scale.

Also contributing to this shift has been the increased focus on the effective use of expatriates. The costs of staffing international sites with expatriates, always high, may now seem unnecessary given the current preference for local management and a team decision making structure. Local managers, who because of education may have been prime expatriate candidates for organizations based in their home country, are also prime candidates for local management for organizations based elsewhere. Global firms based in the US are scouring US business schools for international students who are willing to stay in the US for a few years and then go back to their home country as local managers. Organizations are also thinking of alternative ways to incorporate international experience in their management. They address the pro and cons of several alternatives to expatriation like frequent travel, temporary assignments, or foreign nationals employed on local contracts.

> The value of having lived for a certain period of time in another country is sometimes overestimated: international exposure is different than international success. The adaptability of a British manager flying to China for six weeks several times a year is probably higher than that of a British

manager living in the English speaking community in Brussels. (Interview with M. Avau, 29 June 1993.)

Finally, sufficient numbers of expatriates may simply not be available. Brett and Stroh (1993) report that US managers' willingness to relocate internationally depends upon how their spouses feel about the prospect of an international relocation. Spouses who are not working outside the home and those with children are least likely to be interested in an international relocation.

The multi-cultural managerial workforce is becoming a reality. While the managerial workforces of many US based organizations have become somewhat more diverse in the 1980s due to affirmative action, female and minority managers have been largely confined to lower levels of management (Morrison and Von Glinow, 1990). In contrast, the multi-national local managers, especially those in small, but growing subsidiaries, will quickly move into the ranks of middle management, not because they receive promotions and have middle management titles, but because they will be involved in teams making middle management type decisions.

These teams are already having to confront differences, and not just those due to differences in functional outlook, or local versus global points of view. There are profound and fundamental differences in cultural outlook embedded in a country's social institutions and its citizens' values (Hofstede, 1976, 1980). For instance, the differences in values of individualism versus collectivism and risk versus risk aversion may underlie the negotiators' interests and their preferences for particular negotiation issues (Lytle, 1993). Universalism versus particularism is another cultural value with profound implications for decision making (Trompenaars, 1993). Management policies also may be perceived differently depending on cultural values and societal norms (Janssens, Brett & Smith, 1993).

We have never been impressed by the argument that these cultural differences can be brought into line by a clear organizational vision promulgated by top management. There are three problems with this argument. First, organizational visions change, as well they should, if the organization is to adapt to its ever changing environment. Second, an organizational vision is typically a goal, not a strategy to achieve the goal. Having a clear organizational mission or goal does not mitigate these differences which typically speak to means rather than ends. Third, culture as defined by Schein (1985) consists of different strata with behaviors on the surface, values underlying, and assumptions underlying values. How can an organization coordinate a multi-cultural workforce through creating a "strong" organizational culture when employees' fundamental cultural assumptions clash with those underlying the organization's values and norms?

ALTERNATIVES FOR COORDINATION VIA SOCIALIZATION

Electronic communication, the abandonment of internal labor markets, and the reality of a truly international managerial workforce converge to make coordination based on shared norms and values problematical. The challenge for global corporations is how to coordinate their far-flung businesses under these conditions. We have several suggestions for research and practice.

Electronic Communications

There is a great deal more research to be done on the effects of electronic communications before profound practical recommendations can be made about the most effective use of electronic communications. Among these research issues are:

- Can groups make decisions efficiently and effectively via electronic communications after they have had the opportunity to work together face to face?
- How much face-to-face interaction is needed, and what kind? For example, will experience interacting in management development exercises transfer to strategic decision making via electronic communication?
- Can some group members be linked on-line electronically (text, voice, maybe video) and others face-to-face without losing decision quality?
- What techniques can leaders of groups making decisions via electronic systems use to facilitate consensus? (Kiesler and Sproull (1992) suggest frequent votes.) Will a mixture of on-line conferences, and off-line (when members sign on at different times and may direct communications to specific group members) communications facilitate consensus?
- What are the unanticipated secondary effects of linking global management teams electronically, for an on-line decision making, as well as off-line communications?
- Do electronic systems, because they reduce shared social information, actually aid in reducing differences due to differences in cultural values and in facilitating consensus. Does ignoring differences in cultural values impede implementation of decisions made by group interaction electronically?

Given the current state of the research on electronic communication, we make the following policy suggestions:

- Multi-national, multi-functional groups should be given substantial time to interact face to face.
- These groups should be linked electronically, but not expected to be able to rely on electronic decision making for complex issues involving trade-offs between global and local interests.

Organizational Commitment

When the worldwide economy starts to heat up, corporations may begin to experience the effects of their abandonment of internal labor markets and lifetime employment. Managers in global companies, with their business school degrees and their experience integrating local and global interests, will have the generalizable skills that make them desirable to the external labor market. Their commitment to their careers over their current companies makes them available. The important human resource question is how to maintain international managers' organizational commitment under these circumstances. Can organizational commitment be obtained in another way than through socialization?

The research on turbulence and its effects on managers' attitudes provides some insight. Reilly, Brett and Stroh (1993) found a significant relationship between career loyalty and organizational turbulence, but not between turbulence and corporate loyalty. Their results suggest that those managers who remained with the corporation, despite the turbulence, also remained loyal. These authors discuss alternative explanations for this finding. They recognize that the less loyal managers may have already left the company by the time they collected data, but give this explanation little credence since in the 20 organizations they studied, when an organization had been turbulent, it tended to continue to be. Thus, another explanation is that the managers in their study may have perceived turbulence as a generic condition of the American economy, and not held their organization at fault for instituting various restructuring strategies, especially given they were survivors.

The most compelling explanation and one that squares with these authors' interviews and data from other researchers, however, is that these managers' organizational loyalty came in exchange for fair treatment by the company.

The biggest question for me is "How does the company treat you?"

I think if a company goes through big changes and they treat their people right, it won't affect the way the employees feel. (Interview with Fortune 500 company manager.)

Brockner and his colleagues have found similarly in a series of experiments and field studies (1993) that organizational commitment declined less when layoffs were judged to be handled fairly, than when they were not. In addition, Kim and Mauborgne's studies (1991, 1993) on strategy implementation in multi-national organizations suggest that procedural justice (judgments of the fairness of process) enhances subsidiary managers' attitudes of commitment, trust, outcome satisfaction, and behavior compliance.

The theory of procedural justice distinguishes between fair outcomes and fair process (Thibaut & Walker, 1978). Several important findings from this research are applicable to the problem of maintaining organizational commitment without commitment to internal labor markets and lifetime employment. People report that the decision making process is fair when they feel that they have had some control over the outcome (Shapiro & Brett, 1993; Lind, Kanfer & Early, 1990). People also report that the decision making process is fair when they feel that they have been treated with respect during the process (Lind & Tyler, 1988; Shapiro & Brett, 1993).

Human resources policy relevant to the careers of international managers needs to take both the control and respect elements of procedural justice into consideration. We suggest:

- Make staffing of jobs in the organization's global network a two-way communication process. Use electronic networks to post job and team openings, and encourage people to self nominate.
- Take care to treat managers with global network responsibilities as individuals with unique needs.
- Establish a reciprocal relationship between the manager and the organization. Apply process-oriented training with existing teams as a way to align personal career development and team effectiveness.

There are research issues here as well. The major one turns on how to reward managers for their performance on teams and in groups and committees. Teams, task forces, committees and groups are the current hot structural model not just for managing global organizations' far-flung interests, but also for managing local activities. Yet, commentators avoid discussing how to evaluate them and reward individual members. Hackman (1983) recommends team performance-based rewards be provided equally to all team members. Nadler and Gerstein (1992) similarly argue to create human resource practices that are consistent with autonomous empowered units such as skill-based pay, peer feedback, team bonuses, minimization of rank and hierarchy, and gain sharing.

Team performance-based rewards, however, encourage free riders. Peer evaluation, of course, can identify free riders, but peers may refuse to do so, if they have to continue to work with those individuals in the future.

> I don't think peer evaluation is a good idea. It encourages competition and jealousy. Peer feedback will only work if team assessment happens in the context of training in which no links are made to pay and promotion. (Interview with M. Avau, 29 June 1993.)

Another difficulty is that managers belonging to a team have different objectives. Individuals in cross-functional and cross-hierarchical teams have different lateral and hierarchical links which can create tension within the team or with linked individuals belonging to other groups.

Here is an opportunity for both survey and experimental research.

- What evaluation criteria do managers, whose global network assignments mean they belong to a variety of teams and committees, perceive to be fair?
- Given the different cultural values of the team members, is it fair to reward individuals differently contingent upon the meaning of the rewards?
- Is it fair to compensate individuals on skills especially on those like versatility or promotability? How do these criteria work in practice?
- Is there a way to integrate the different, possibly conflicting, objectives? Who do managers perceive to be a fair assessor of the different inputs?

The Multi-Cultural Managerial Workforce

The multi-cultural managerial workforce, organized into teams and linked electronically, is likely to make coordination more difficult. Traditionally, heterogeneity and conflict were seen as undesirable. Several authors have argued that a strong culture with a homogeneous workforce would contribute to the overall effectiveness of an organization (e.g. Deal & Kennedy, 1982; Peters & Waterman, 1982). Nowadays, multiple inputs and perspectives are seen as essential for creative decision making, and innovative, adaptable functioning. The question, then, becomes how to manage the differences that a multi-cultural managerial workforce brings to organizations.

A first step is for managers to become aware of their differences in behavior, values, and fundamental assumptions. A second step is for managers to recognize that argument is not going to make these differences disappear. It is essential for managers to learn that they are going to have coexist with others who behave differently, and have different values and assumptions. Finally, managers must be willing to consider different perspectives when making decisions.

> Managers in intercultural teams have different values. Leaders of a multicultural team often favor a uniform way in motivating and rewarding managers but I advise an open discussion about differences in priorities and appreciations. The management of multi-cultural teams needs to be characterized by variety. (Interview with M. Avau, 29 June 1993.)

Awareness does not resolve the coordination problem. How can managers consider conflicting perspectives and still coordinate their activities? We believe that managers need skills in confronting and transcending their differences, skills in negotiating that take into account the different perspectives which dominate different parts of the company in different areas of the world. A team of managers has intelligence which individual managers lack. The ultimate goal is to reconcile the differences they bring to a problem synergistically (Hampden-Turner, 1990).

Our recommendations for training to prepare multi-national teams and managers to deal with their differences are:

- There is a role for traditional team building in which members become aware of each other's differences, know each other's strengths and weaknesses, and trust each other to cooperate when an individual has the option to go it alone.
- Training in mental management in which managers are learning reframing and third party intervention skills such as two-way communication, integrative negotiation skills that encourage win–win strategies, and broker's skills (Steyaert & Janssens, 1993).
- Training in integrative and distributive negotiation skills in dyads as well as in groups, especially when negotiators come from different cultures and use different tactics and strategies.

We note that research has shown that when groups of individualistically oriented members vote frequently on multi-issue proposals, they perform as well as groups of cooperative members (Weingart, Bennett & Brett, 1993). Furthermore, frequent voting is one of the techniques Kiesler and Sproull (1992) recommend to help electronic groups making decisions. There is substantial research to be done to further understanding of how to manage differences and negotiate in inter-functional, inter-national groups, both when they are working in a face-to-face context and whey they are linked electronically. Among these research issues are:

- How to facilitate high quality, integrative group decisions when some group members are cooperative and some are individualistically oriented?
- Do groups reach equally high quality decisions when negotiating electronically as face-to-face when required to take frequent votes?
- How are multi-cultural teams best led? Should leadership be different when the group is working electronically versus face to face?

CONCLUSION

The challenge of coordinating the far-flung enterprises of global companies in the light of current developments in electronic communications, organizational commitment, and a multi-cultural managerial workforce provides opportunities to apply some fundamental knowledge from psychology and to inspire fundamental research. With assets and resources widely dispersed, with decisions requiring the balancing of global economies with local needs, and the diffusion of innovation necessary for survival, global companies have little choice but to develop new ways of coordinating. We think that reliance on electronic communication will have to be supplemented with human resource policies that emphasize fairness and the coexistence of differences, as well as the development of managerial skills to deal with these differences.

ACKNOWLEDGMENT

The authors would like to thank Dr M. Avau, Training Manager ICI, for her suggestions.

REFERENCES

Baglioni, G. & Crouch, C. (Eds.) (1990) *European Industrial Relations: The Challenge of Flexibility*. London: Sage.
Bartlett, C. A. & Ghoshal, S. (1989) *Managing Across Borders: The Transnational Solution*. Cambridge, MA: Harvard University Press.
Bartlett, C. A. & Ghoshal, S. (1990). Matrix management: Not a structure, a frame of mind. *Harvard Business Review*, July–August, 138–145.

Blyton, P. & Morris, J. (1992) HRM and the limits of flexibility. In P. Blyton & P. Turnbull (Eds.) *Reassessing Human Resource Management*. London: Sage, pp. 116–130.

Brett, J. M. & Stroh, L. K. (1993) Willingness to relocate internationally. Working Paper, Northwestern University, J. L. Kellogg Graduate School of Management, Evanston.

Brockner, J., Grover, T., O'Malley, M., Reed, T. & Glynn, M. (1993) Threat of future layoffs, self-esteem, and survivors' reactions: Evidence from the laboratory and the field. *Strategic Management Journal*, **14**, 153–166.

Deal, T. E. & Kennedy, A. A. (1982) *Corporate Cultures*. Reading, MA: Addison-Wesley.

Gerstein, M. S. & Shaw, R. B. (1992) Organizational architectures for the twenty-first century. In D. A. Nadler, M. S. Gerstein, R. B. Shaw, and Associates (Eds.) *Organizational Architecture: Designs for Changing Organizations*. New York: Jossey-Bass, pp. 263–273.

Hackman, J. R. (1983) Designing work for individuals and for groups. In J. R. Hackman, E. E. Lawler III, and L. W. Porter (Eds.) *Perspectives on Behavior in Organizations*. New York: McGraw Hill, pp. 242–258.

Hampden-Turner, C. (1990) *Charting the Corporate Mind: Graphic Solutions to Business Conflicts*. New York: Collier.

Hirsch, P. (1987) *Pack Your Own Parachute*. Reading, MA: Addison-Wesley.

Hofstede, G. (1976) Nationality and the espoused values of managers. *Journal of Applied Psychology*, **61**, 148–155.

Hofstede, G. (1980) *Culture's Consequences: National Differences in Thinking and Organizing*. Beverley Hills, CA: Sage.

Janssens, M., Brett, J. M. & Smith, F. J. (1993) Managing safety across cultures. Working Paper, Northwestern University, J. L. Kellogg Graduate School of Management, Evanston.

Kiesler, S. & Sproull, L. (1992) Group decision making and communication technology. *Organizational Behavior and Human Decision Processes*, **52**, 96–123.

Kim, W. C. & Mauborgne, R. A. (1991) Implementing global strategies: The role of procedural justice. *Strategic Management Journal*, **12**, 125–143.

Kim, W. C. & Mauborgne, R. A. (1993) Procedural justice, attitudes, and subsidiary top management compliance with multinationals' corporate strategic decisions. *Academy of Management Journal*, **36**(3), 502–526.

Lind, E. A. & Tyler, T. (1988) *The Social Psychology of Procedural Justice*. New York: Plenum.

Lind, E. A., Kanfer, R. & Early, P. C. (1990) Voice, control, and procedural justice: Instrumental and noninstrumental concerns in fairness judgments. *Journal of Personality and Social Psychology*, **59**, 952–959.

Lytle, A. L. (1993) The influence of culture in negotiations: the case of negotiator interests. *Working Paper*, Northwestern University, J. L. Kellogg Graduate School of Management, Evanston.

Manichi Daily News (1993) Geen baan meer voot het leven [No job for life anymore]. In *Manpower Argus, News about work and the world of work* (Ed. Manpower Europe), 68, June, p. 4.

Morrison, A. M. & Von Glinow, M. A. (1990) Women and minorities in management. *American Psychologist*, **45**, 200–208.

Nadler, D. A. & Gerstein, M. S. (1992) Designing high-performance work systems: Organizing people, work, technology, and information. In D. A. Nadler, M. S. Gerstein, R. B. Shaw and Associates (Eds.) *Organizational*

Architecture: Designs for Changing Organizations. New York: Jossey-Bass, pp. 110–132.

Nordström, K. (1993) The `global' management of European business. Paper presented at *Colloquium: Cultural Differences, Management & Economics,* Organised by Vlerick School of Management, September 18, Brussels.

OECD (Organisation for Economic Cooperation and Development) (Ed.) (1989) *Labour Market Flexibility: Trends in Enterprises.* Paris: OECD.

Peters, T. J. & Waterman, R. H. (1982) *In Search of Excellence.* New York: Harper & Row.

Reed, M. & Hughes, M. (1992) *Rethinking Organizations.* London: Sage.

Reilly, A. H., Brett, J. M. & Stroh, L. K. (1993) The impact of corporate turbulence on managers' attitudes. *Strategic Management Journal,* **14,** 167–179.

Shapiro, D. & Brett, J. M. (1993) Comparing three processes underlying judgments of procedural justice: A filed study of mediation and arbitration. *Journal of Personality and Social Psychology,* **65,** 1167–1177.

Schein, E. H. (1985) *Organisational Culture and Leadership.* London: Jossey-Bass.

Snow, C. C., Miles, R. E. & Coleman, H. J. (1992) Managing 21st century network organizations. *Organizational Dynamics,* Winter, 5–20.

Sonnenfeld, J. A. & Peiperl, M. A. (1988) Staffing policy as a strategic response: A typology of career systems. *Academy of Management Review,* **13**(4), 588–600.

Steyaert, C. & Janssens, M. (1993) The world in two and a way out: The concept of duality in organization theory and practice. *Working Paper,* Katholieke Universiteit Leuven, Belgium.

The Economist (1993) Einde van trouw aan het bedrijf [The end of organizational loyalty]. In *Manpower Argus, News about work and the world of work.* (Ed. Manpower Europe), 68, June, p.7.

Thibaut, J. & Walker, L. (1978) *A theory of Procedural Justice.* Hillsdale, NJ: Erlbaum.

Trompenaars, F. (1993) *Riding the Waves of Culture: Understanding Cultural Diversity in Business.* London: The Economists Books.

Walton, R. E. (1985) From control to commitment in the workplace. *Harvard Business Review,* March–April, 77–84.

Weingart, L. R., Bennett, R. J. & Brett, J. M. (1993) The impact of consideration of issues and motivational orientation on group negotiation process and outcome. *Journal of Applied Psychology,* **78,** 504–517.

Weisband, S. P. (1992) Group discussion and first advocacy effects in computer-mediated and face-to-face decision making groups. *Organizational Behavior and Human Decision Making Processes,* **53**(3), 352–380.

CHAPTER 4

The Human Effects of Mergers and Acquisitions

Sue Cartwright and Cary L. Cooper

University of Manchester, Institute of Science and Technology, UK

INTRODUCTION

The merger mania of the 1980s seemed to have lost its impetus as the business world entered a new decade and the gloom of global recession. From an all time peak in 1988, the rate of US and UK merger and acquisition (M & A) activity began to decline as many organizations moved to "downsize" rather than "upsize" their operations. In periods of recession and market uncertainty, caution dictates that organizational concern will tend to focus on "hanging on in there" and maintaining the existing customer base rather than embarking on any major expansion programme involving corporate acquisition. Commonsensically, why take the risk of borrowing heavily and increasing gearing ratios to acquire a less financially robust competitor, whom, if the recession continues to bite, is likely to quietly disappear anyway?

Given the available research evidence on M & A performance, the reluctance to engage in this type of high risk activity would seem to be well founded, irrespective of the external economic climate which may be operating. M & A success can be defined and measured in a variety of ways (Hogan & Overmyer-Day, 1994; Cartwright & Cooper, 1992). Financial performance is taken to be the most common indicator of M & A success. This can be measured objectively in terms of share price fluctuations, profit–earnings ratios, net income etc., or by the subjective assessments of managers, financial commentators and/or City analysts.

Trends in Organizational Behavior, Volume 1. Edited by C. L. Cooper and D. M. Rousseau
© 1994 John Wiley & Sons Ltd.

However, increasingly the success of any organizational combination has been gauged by the reactions of the individuals affected. This has involved the use of behavioral indices to assess success in terms of the impact the event has had on employee outcomes such as labor turnover, job satisfaction, commitment, stress and affective response.

It will be recognized that the extensive range of criteria by which M & A success can be assessed, coupled with the inherent difficulties in deciding the appropriate period of time over which to make that measurement, presents many problems. There appears to be a developing consensus towards a two year period (Hogan & Overmyer-Day, 1994).

However, evidence based on M and A experiences during the 1980s and the previous boom of the 1960s, regardless of whether this emanates from the so-called "hard" (i.e. financial data) or "soft" (i.e. behavioral data) sources, is consistent in its disappointing analysis and prognosis of future M & A success. Estimates of M & A failure range from a pessimistic 80% (Marks, 1988; Ellis & Pekar, 1978; Kitching, 1967) to a more optimistic, yet still disappointing 50% (Cartwright & Cooper, 1992; Porter, 1987; British Institute of Management, 1986; Young, 1981). Furthermore, failure rates appear to be little moderated by previous experience (Hunt, 1987), in that seasoned acquirers are unlikely to outperform novices. However, it has been suggested (Jemison & Sitkin, 1986) that organizations which have acquired or merged in the past are more likely to consider issues relating to the cultural and psychological match between the workforces.

Recent upturns in the economy appear to have caused a resurgence in business confidence. As recessionary gloom starts to lift, certain organizations have survived to emerge in a rather better state of financial health than others. The implications are clear. The potential growth benefits to be gained from M & A once again exercise a persuasive and seductive appeal to organizations, particularly when there are likely to be "bargains" around. At the same time, the motive to merge is also inclined to strengthen amongst financially vulnerable organizations as a defense against the possible threat of a hostile takeover bid. Combined, these factors are likely to create an increasing pool of potential buyers and sellers, and a rise in M & A activity. The evidence would seem to confirm this to be the situation. According to recent reports (Cartwright & Cooper, 1993c), M & A activity has started to pick up. In the first six months of 1993, the number of M & A's showed an increase of 30% compared with the same period in the previous year.

If, as predicted, this upward trend seems set to continue, the burning issue for those involved in M & A decisions and integration management is the extent to which there are helpful lessons to be learnt from the past which can usefully be applied to improve M & A success rates. The aim of this chapter is to consolidate the findings of existing research which has addressed the human aspects of M & A, and discuss their implications for more proactive and effective management of such corporate alliances in the 1990s. The intention of this chapter is not to present an extensive scholarly review of the OB literature in this field, for this, the reader is directed to other existing sources (e.g. Hogan & Overmyer-Day, 1994; Cartwright & Cooper, 1990; Napier, 1989). Its purpose is to focus on a number of salient issues arising from research which are relevant to managerial practice. Although it is recognized that as mergers and acquisitions are legally different transactions, mergers are rarely a marriage between equals (Humpal, 1971) in terms of their impact on the vast majority of the employees involved. The two terms, however, are treated synonymously throughout this chapter.

The bulk of the literature relating to M & A's still continues to focus on economic, financial and strategic factors rather than human factors; particularly as they concern target or partner selection. Typically, M & A failure has been attributed to over inflated purchase prices, lack of strategic fit, subsequent financial mismanagement or incompetence. As has been suggested (Cartwright & Cooper, 1993b), this ground has been well trodden, but still remains inadequate in accounting for the range of negative behavioral outcomes associated with the event, such as high voluntary attrition rates (Walsh, 1988; Unger, 1986), absenteeism (Davey et al, 1988), widescale disruption and unproductive behavior (Sinetar, 1981) employee stress (Cartwright & Cooper, 1993a) and unprecedented acts of sabotage and petty theft (Altendorf, 1986). All of which are likely to impact upon the performance of the combination and are subsequently reflected in "the bottom line".

M & A's are complex human as well as financial phenomena. Balance sheet explanations of disappointing financial results often mask or ignore the human contribution required to make a combination successful. A fairly recent estimate (Davey et al, 1988) attributed "employee problems" as being responsible for between one-third to a half of all merger failures. A survey of over 200 European chief executives (Booz, Allen & Hamilton, 1985) found that "ability to integrate the new company" was ranked as a significantly more important factor than "price paid". According to Marks (1988), M & A's differ from any other organizational change in three important aspects: the speed of change, the scale of change and the critical mass of the unknown they present for both parties. Based on recent empirical research in this area, Cartwright and Cooper (1992) concluded that M &

A's present a distinct and special challenge to management. The main reasons being:

- M & A's are emotive and potentially stressful events which affect almost everybody involved.
- M & A's create an expectancy of change and increase intraorganizational cohesiveness.
- M & A management teams are invariably overconfident in their estimation of the speed and ease with which they can achieve integration.
- M & A's result in unplanned personnel losses at all levels, which, apart from the loss of talent such departures may represent, also have a disruptive and demotivating effect on those who remain.

Characteristically, the problems of human resource management, inherent in M & A situations, concern dealing with employee uncertainty, maintaining motivation and overcoming resistance to change. Whilst these are salient issues in all M & A's, the scale and degree to which these problems manifest themselves and the way in which they can be more effectively managed are moderated by two important variables: (i) the degree of cultural fit which exists between the combining organizations and (ii) the objectives and type of organizational marriage envisaged by the two corporate parties.

ORGANIZATIONAL FIT

A distinction can be drawn between making a merger or acquisition decision and making a merger or acquisition work (Jemison & Sitkin, 1986). The former is concerned with the selection process (i.e. recognizing the synergistic potential), and the latter with the management of the integration process (i.e. releasing that potential). In practice, the responsibilities for these two aspects usually lies with different managerial groups.

In terms of selection, both the strategic and organizational fit are considered to be important determinants of M & A success. Strategic fit concerns shared or complementary business strategies and financial goals. Organizational fit is considered to relate to the degree to which the partnering organizations are matched in terms of their administrative systems and procedures, demographic characteristics, managerial style and corporate cultures.

The issue of cultural fit has increasingly become a strong theme in the more recent literature relating to M & A's. There is a considerable amount of anecdotal reporting and a limited, but hopefully developing, body of empirical research (Buono, Bowditch & Lewis, 1985; Cartwright & Cooper, 1992) to indicate that differences in corporate culture influence perceptions and expectations of M & A, and serve to create ambiguous and often hostile working environments. A survey of over 150 managers involved in the "friendly" merger of two savings and loan institutions (Cartwright & Cooper, 1993a) suggests that at the time of a merger, intraorganizational cohesiveness increases to such an ethnocentric extent that even when the two cultures are extremely similar, employees may fail to recognize this.

Poor cultural fit or lack of cultural compatibility has consistently been blamed for unsatisfactory merger outcomes and is hypothesized as being responsible for the high disposal or "divorce" rates. Walter (1985) estimates that the cost of culture collisions resulting from poor integration may be as high as 25–30% of the performance of the acquired company. Press reports surrounding the "friendly" merger of Connecticut General and the Insurance Company of North America into CIGNA in March 1982 linked the 10% decline in operating income during the first year to the very different cultural values and expectations held by the two workforces and the problems which occurred as a result. Based on a review of almost thirty major studies on merger performance, Hall and Norburn (1987) suggested two interesting hypotheses:

- That the degree of cultural fit which exists between the two combining organizations will be directly correlated with the financial success of the venture.
- Where a lack of culture fit exists, success will be determined by the degree of autonomy afforded to the two operations.

Unfortunately, until recently (Cartwright & Cooper, 1992, 1993b; Nahavandi & Malekzadeh, 1988) the lack of an effective framework or model for assessing and evaluating what exactly constitutes a good "culture fit" has made any operational testing of these hypotheses extremely difficult.

Recent research into acquirer behavior (Hunt, 1988; Cartwright & Cooper, 1992) confirms a continued lack of "information gathering" on the issue of organizational/culture fit prior to deal completion. It still remains the case that while acquiring or merging organizations are well informed as to the financial and legal health of their acquisition target or merger partner, any form of pre-formation human resource or culture audit is a rare occurrence. This is despite evidence to suggest that the more successful acquisitions and joint ventures are likely to be made by those organizations which are well informed about their partner (Hunt, 1988). Typically, the assessment of the potential culture fit between two organizations, if at all considered, is generally intuitive and based on information gained from interactions between the negotiating teams. Such information is likely to be limited, as negotiations rarely involve the personnel function and frequently involve individuals or agencies who have a financial stake in seeing the deal go through (McManus & Hergert, 1988). Even if culture differences do become apparent, these often only come to light at a time when so much energy has been expended in negotiation that "reluctance to withdraw" is so strong that it is more convenient to ignore or dismiss them. However, recent UK press reports surrounding the decision made by the Leeds Permanent and the National & Provincial Building Societies to withdraw from merger negotiations attribute the reason for the non-consummation to recognized cultural differences between the parties.

Characteristically, negotiations focus on establishing shared objectives (the what is to be achieved) at the expense of implementation or process issues (the how it is to be achieved). As a result, it has increasingly become the practice for large organizations subsequently faced with integration or process problems to call upon external management consultants to sort out the so-called "teething problems". If only, from the outset, the impulse to "call in the auditors" was applied with similar enthusiasm and celerity to human resource and OB specialists.

Better and more proactive management of the human aspects of M & A's, therefore, should begin at the decision making stage, by devoting equal time and resources to the issue of organizational/cultural fit in order to select more compatible partners. Hogan and Overmyer-Day (1994) suggest that culture clash issues can be alleviated by well designed conflict resolution mechanisms, open-culture related communication and recognition of the time needed for acculturation. Cartwright and Cooper (1992) advocate that organizations make better use of available pre-acquisition information; with regard to the company's history, background and corporate policy, attend more to the negotiation style, campaign for more involvement of the personnel function and if possible conduct some form of culture audit. Rankine (1991) emphasizes the value of conducting customer as well as competitor research. Given the possible limitation of access, another possible technique in culture assessment, along the lines of situational interviews, would be to present the negotiating team with a number of potential scenarios and invite their comments as to possible action/response.

TYPES OF MARRIAGE

Commenting on the merger boom of the 1960s, Levinson (1970) drew the useful analogy between merger and marriage, whereby the compatibility of the partners is considered crucial to the success of the combination. This analogy has been a recurrent theme of much of the later literature (Humpal, 1971; Mangham, 1973; Jick, 1979; Cartwright & Cooper, 1992), and is consistent with the notion of culture match or fit.

Selecting an appropriate merger partner is not dissimilar from selecting a life partner. Both activities tend to be characterized by a high degree of initial optimism, a certain "blindness" to any undesirable qualities in the other, or at least a confident, sometimes arrogant belief that any differences are not insurmountable and will be resolved, as one partner learns to adapt to the other post combination (Jemison & Sitkin, 1986; Cartwright & Cooper, 1992). Definitions as to what constitutes partner compatibility in terms of an organizational marriage is as complex an issue as in civil marriages. Given that both forms of marriage tend to record similarly high rates of failure and dissolution, it raises the question, does compatibility mean being similar or being different but complementary?

Dependent upon the degree to which the business activities of the combining organizations are related, M & A's are generally classified into four main types:

- *Vertical*—combinations between two organizations from successive processes within the same industry.
- *Horizontal*—combinations between organizations in the same industry.
- *Conglomerate*—combinations between organizations in completely unrelated areas of business activity.
- *Concentric*—combinations in an unfamiliar but related field.

A further distinction is often drawn in terms of the degree of friendliness which exists between the two partners (Hunt, 1988). Such typologies influence the degree of physical, procedural and socio-cultural integration considered necessary to achieve financial and strategic objectives and partner attitudes. During the boom of the 1960s most M & A's were of the conglomerate type; in contrast, during the 1980s the trend has been towards horizontal combinations. Nahavandi and Malekzadeh (1988) propose that the cultural dynamics of a M & A are a reflection or outcome of the process of adaptation and acculturation. Acculturation is an anthropological term, generally defined as "changes introduced in (two cultural) systems as a result of the diffusion of cultural elements in both directions". Although this suggests a balanced two way flow, Berry (1980) states that members of one culture frequently attempt to dominate members of the other. This is likely to occur in any type of M & A, but especially in horizontal combinations where the acquirer or dominant or larger merger partner has established experience of the industry and product market in which the other operates. Dependent upon the willingness of organizational members to abandon their existing culture and their perceptions of the attractiveness of "the other" culture, it is proposed that acculturation can take four possible modes (Figure 4.1).

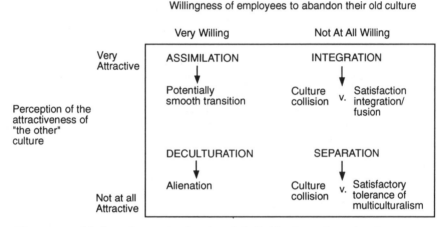

Figure 4.1 Modes of organizational and individual acculturation in mergers and acquisitions and their potential outcomes. (Adapted from Nahavandi & Malekzadeh, 1988)

It has been suggested (Cartwright & Cooper, 1993b) that the issue of cultural compatibility can be understood within the framework of this model, if account is taken of the type and implicit terms of the organizational marriage or partnership agreement. They propose three possible types or forms a marriage can take, depending upon the motive, objective and power dynamics of the combination (Table 4.1).

Based on empirical research in this area, Cartwright and Cooper (1992) concluded that most organizational marriages are of the traditional type, or at least are initially responded to by the majority of employees as being so. Consequently, the pre-existing culture types of the combination and the direction of culture change are crucial in determining the response of organizational members and the degree of resistance to change. These findings, based on precombination assessment using the typology originally proposed by Harrison (1972, 1987), suggested that successful assimilation was likely to occur in situations where the culture

Table 4.1 Three possible types of partnership

Type	Characterized by:	Terms
Open marriage	Satisfaction with present performance of partner/acquired organization and/or confidence in existing management Partner sees its role as being supportive and further facilitating the growth and development of the other without overt interference Tolerance of multi-culturation	The acquired organization is sanctioned to maintain cultural *separation* and operate autonomously provided it meets expected target(s) Minimal changes—possible integration of reporting systems and procedures
Traditional marriage	Dissatisfaction with present performance and/or existing management Partner sees its role as being one of radical redesign and the introduction of wide scale change	The acquired or the "other merger partner" is required to totally adopt and *assimilate* into the practice, procedures and culture of the acquirer or dominant merger partner
Modern or collaborative marriage	High degree of respect between the parties and a genuine recognition that the integration of operations and/or exchange of expertise will ultimately be of mutual benefit A commitment to shared learning	A meaningful commitment to cultural *integration* to create a "best of both worlds" culture and exchange of best practice

of the acquirer or dominant partner is perceived as likely to reduce individual constraints and increase autonomy. Loss of managerial autonomy is frequently cited as a major reason for voluntary decisions to leave acquired or merged organizations (Hayes & Hoag, 1974) and rated as significantly more important than changes in pay and benefits.

Other researchers (Krupar & Krupar, 1988; Datta, 1991) have similarly identified power and control mechanisms, and the degree of decision making responsibility, as key areas where cultural clashes are likely to occur, particularly where a high degree of integration is necessary to achieve M & A objectives, as in horizontal combinations. In contrast, differences in culture in areas such as reward and evaluation systems have not been found to be predictors of subsequent M & A performance (Datta, 1991).

The value of conducting some form of culture audit either on or immediately post merger is advocated (Cartwright & Cooper, 1992) as a means of anticipating future problems, perhaps by renegotiation or clarification of the marriage terms. Culture audits could also be used to monitor the ongoing process of integration.

EMPLOYEE RESPONSE TO M & A

M & A's represent large scale and often sudden organizational change, and consequently create considerable uncertainty amongst employees. It was estimated that during the 1980s at least one in four of the US workforce were likely to have been affected by M & A activity (Fulmer, 1986). As M & A's are associated with rationalization, personnel changes, disrupted career prospects, alterations in working practices and culture, loss of identity and status, lack of information and secrecy, they are perceived to have a threatening and destabilizing effect on employees producing "a painful social psychological ripple" felt by almost all organizational members (Jick, 1979).

The psychological response of employees to a M & A announcement has frequently been compared with the sense of loss experienced following bereavement (Ivancevich, Schweiger & Power, 1987; Marks & Mirvis, 1986; Mirvis, 1985). It is often remembered with the vividness associated with "flashbulb" type memories (Sinetar, 1981). Within the framework of the Kubler-Ross model of bereavement (Kubler-Ross, 1969), it is postulated that employee reactions will pass through four stages; Disbelief and Denial, Anger, Emotional Bargaining and Depression, and finally Acceptance. Fixation at any of the earlier stages is likely to result in preoccupation and unproductive behavior, or may cause the individual to leave the organization. Sufficient research is available about loss more generally to posit that it produces a conservative and nostalgic impulse in individuals to hold on to what they have (Mirvis, 1985; Buono, Bowditch & Lewis III, 1985). Furthermore, collective grief is likely to increase cohesiveness and resistance to change, and make new cultures and managerial practices even more difficult to introduce.

The uncertainty and feelings of loss of control triggered by the M & A event are likely to lead to widescale anxiety and stress, even amongst acquiring management (Mangham, 1973). Whilst the human and financial costs of occupational stress generally are well documented, until recently (Cartwright & Cooper, 1993a), it had been little considered in accounting for merger failure. Stress research in the context of major intraorganizational change (Ashford, 1988) suggests that such events are universally stressful and little moderated by personality characteristics.

Cultural transitions which result in ambiguous or fragmented cultures have also been shown to affect mental health adversely (Cartwright & Cooper, 1989); continuing for some appreciable time and with a significantly pronounced effect on employees of the target company or smaller merger partner (Cartwright & Cooper, 1993a). Hunsaker and Coombs (1988) suggest that the degree of hostility and conflict between the combining organizations will also influence the degree of experienced stress. The availability of alternative job opportunities and domestic circumstances are also likely to play a role. Control is recognized to be an important variable in the stress equation, as has been found (Hunsaker & Coombs, 1988) with senior managers, who are closer to the decision making process and are more likely therefore to experience relatively less stress than those at lower levels. Increased organizational size in itself has been shown to reduce organizational commitment and perceptions of influence.

According to Schweiger and Ivancevich (1985) stress arises more from the perceptions which employees have as to the likely changes which may result rather than the actual changes themselves. They suggest that the presentation of a realistic merger preview (RMP) is likely to be useful in enabling employees to make realistic, cognitive appraisals. RMPs are similar to realistic job previews (Wanous, 1980), in that their aim is to provide employees with a clear and unambiguous picture of what they can expect the "new" organization to be like.

It is recommended that a RMP is presented in the early stages post merger/acquisition in the form of a film, booklet or group presentation. The provision of RMPs and merger related communication has been demonstrated to have a significant impact on job satisfaction and employee perceptions of organizational honesty, caring and trustworthiness, compared with situations when such information was absent or minimal (Schweiger & DeNisi, 1991). Interestingly, on the basis of this study, the act of communicating itself may be as important as, if not more important than, the content.

Whilst the importance of communication is emphasized throughout the OB merger literature, in itself it is not a panacea for all M & A problems and may, as has been suggested (Robino & DeMeuse, 1985), increase hostility between merging workforces. In the context of reducing stress, open communication is likely to be effective in the early stages, but may need to be supplemented by more specific stress management initiatives, individual counselling and retraining programmes to improve employee coping skills. The formation of joint working parties or merger integration teams or the introduction of quality circle types initiatives is likely to increase employee feelings of fairness and involvement, and thus restore a sense of control. This is particularly pertinent in the area of merger reselection decisions.

It would seem that dealing effectively with employee stress may initially require a strongly overt organizational initiative. M & A's are unprecedented events for most employees and so they are unlikely to have developed an effective coping strategy (Schweiger & Ivancevich, 1985). Mergers are highly emotive events in organizational life, in which employees are understandably likely to feel reluctant to express their anxieties for fear of jeopardizing their career prospects. Mangham (1973) in describing the interpersonal relationships between the Ever-so-Smooth Cosmetics–Crocodile Chemicals merger found that managers who voiced objections to post acquisition changes were labelled as "resistant to change". This label was considered to be a "fate worse than death", because those so labelled were subsequently replaced. Marks (1988) states that one of the common characteristics of the merger situation is a fear on the part of executives to expose any sign of vulnerability and give any indication that one is not tough enough for the postmerger organization. The pressure to appear outwardly "merger fit" and willing and able to change may, therefore, lead to long term dysfunctional stress which otherwise could be addressed and possibly avoided.

SUMMARY

Many of the problems associated with M & A's stem from poor initial selection decisions with regard to organizational or cultural fit. However, irrespective of this issue, when an organization ceases to exist or is fundamentally changed, the psychological contract—the expectations that the individuals has of the other—is broken, becomes unclear and has to be re-established or negotiated. Because M and A's create uncertainty and are experienced by employees as unprecedented circumstances over which they have little or no control, they are inherently stressful. The emotional and behavioral manifestations of stress are potentially dysfunctional to both individual well-being and organizational outcomes. The major sources of stress generally tend to be job security and work overload. The reduction and longer term management of merger stress, together with initiatives to increase employee participation to restore a sense of control, are likely to be key elements in merger success.

It is recognized that M & A's are particularly difficult areas for researchers to gain access to. Simulated laboratory studies or quasi-merger situations (Berney, 1986; Humpal, 1971) are poor substitutes for the dynamics of the "real life" situation.

In recent years, the OB literature has moved away from its speculative anecdotal and prescriptive approach to M & A's, and become more research/theory driven. However, the development of comprehensive and testable models for understanding such an important and complex aspect of corporate activity is still in its infancy, and it is an area where more systematic and longitudinal research is needed.

REFERENCES

Altendorf, D. M. (1986) When cultures clash: a case study of the Texaco takeover of Getty Oil and the impact of acculturation on the acquired firm. August 1986, PhD Dissertation, Faculty of Graduate School of Business Administrator, University of Southern California.

Ashford, S. J. (1988) Individual strategies for coping with stress during organisational transitions. *Journal of Applied Behavioural Science*, **24**(1), 19–26.

Berney, E. J. (1986) Management decision-making in acquisitions—an intergroup analysis" *PhD Theses Abstracts International, No 86*—14199 Ann Arbor, Michigan.

Berry, J. W. (1980) Social and cultural change. In H. C. Triandis & R. W. Brislin (Eds.) *Handbook of Cross Cultural Psychology*, **5**, 211–279, Allyn & Bacon, Boston.

Booz, Allen & Hamilton Inc. (1985) *Diversification: A Survey of European Chief Executives—Executive Summary*. Booz, Allen & Hamilton: New York.

British Institute of Management (1986) *The Management of Acquisitions and Mergers*. Discussion Paper No. 8, Economics Department, September.

Buono, A. F., Bowditch, J. L. & Lewis III, J. W. (1985) When cultures collide: the anatomy of a merger. *Human Relations*, **38**(5), 477–500.

Cartwright, S. & Cooper, C. L. (1989) Predicting success in joint venture organisations in information technology—a cultural perspective. *Journal of General Management*, **15**, 39–52.

Cartwright, S. & Cooper, C. L. (1990) The impact of mergers and acquisitions on people at work: Existing research and issues. *British Journal of Management*, **1**, 65–76.

Cartwright, S. & Cooper, C. L. (1992) *Mergers and Acquisitions: The Human Factor*. Oxford: Butterworth & Heinemann.

Cartwright, S. & Cooper, C. L. (1993a) The psychological impact of merger and acquisition on the individual: a study of building society managers. *Human Relations*, **46**(3), 327–347.

Cartwright, S. & Cooper, C. L. (1993b) The role of culture compatibility in successful organisational marriage. *Academy of Management Executive*, **7**(2), 57–70.

Cartwright, S. & Cooper, C. L. (1993c) If cultures don't fit, mergers mail fail. *New York Times*, August 29.

Datta, D. K. (1991) Organisational fit and acquisition performance: effects of post acquisition integration. *Strategic Management Journal*, **12**, 281–297.

Davy, J. A., Kinicki, A., Kilroy, J. & Scheck, C. (1988) After the merger: dealing with people's uncertainty. *Training & Development Journal*, November, 57–61.

Ellis, D. J. & Pekar, P. P. (1978) Acquisitions: is 50/50 good enough? *Planning Review*, **(6)** 4, July 15–19.

Fulmer, R. (1986) Meeting the merger integration challenge with management development. *Journal of Management Development*, **5**, Part 4, 7–16.

Hall, P. D. & Norburn, D. (1987) The management factor in acquisition performance. *Leadership and Organisational Development Journal*, **8**(3), 23–30.

Harrison, R. (1972) How to describe your organisation. *Harvard Business Review*, May/June **5**/1, 119–128.

Harrison, R. (1987) *Organisational Culture and the Quality of Service*. London: Association for Management Education and Development.

Hayes, R. H. & Hoag, G. H. (1974) Post acquisition retention of top management. *Mergers & Acquisitions*, **9**, 8–18.

Hogan, E. & Overmyer-Day, L. (1994) The psychology of mergers and acquisitions. In C. L. Cooper & I. T. Robertson (Eds.) *International Review of Industrial and Organisational Psychology*, **9**, 247–279.

Humpal, J. J. (1971) Organisational marriage counselling: A first step. *Journal of Applied Behavioural Science*, **7**, 103–109.

Hunsaker, P. L. & Coombs, M. W. (1988) Mergers & acquisitions: managing the emotional issues. *Personnel Journal*, **65**, 56–63.

Hunt, J. (1987) Hidden extras—how people get overlooked in takeovers. *Personnel Management*, July, 24–26.

Hunt, J. (1988) Managing the successful acquisition: A people question. *London Business School Journal*, Summer, 2–15.

Ivancevich, J. M., Schweiger, D. M. & Power, F. R. (1987) Strategies for managing human resources during mergers and acquisitions. *Human Resource Planning*, **12**, part 1, (Mar), 19–35.

Jemison, D. & Sitkin, S. B. (1986) Corporate acquisitions: a process perspective. *Academy of Management Review*, **11**(1), 145–163.

Jick, T. D. (1979) Processes and impact of a merger; individual and organisational perspectives. Unpublished doctoral dissertation, Cornell University.

Kitching, J. (1967) "Why do mergers miscarry?" *Harvard Business Review*, Nov/Dec.

Krupar, K. R. & Krupar, J. J. (1988) Consider the people-fit issues during mergers. *Personnel Journal*, March 1988, 95–98.

Kubler-Ross, E. (1969) *On Death and Dying*. New York: MacMillan.

Levinson, H. (1970) A psychologist diagnoses merger failures. *Harvard Business Review*, March/April, 84–101.

Mangham, I. (1973) Facilitating intraorganisational dialogue in a merger situation. *Journal of Interpersonal Development*, **4**, 133–147.

Marks, M. L. (1988) The merger syndrome: The human side of corporate combinations. *Journal of Buyouts and Acquisitions*, Jan./Feb., 18–23.

Marks, M. L. & Mirvis, P. H. (1986) The merger syndrome. *Psychology Today*, October 20, (10), 36–42.

McManus, M. L. & Hergert, M. L. (1988) *Surviving Merger and Acquisition*. Scott Foresman: Glenview, Illinois.

Mirvis, P. H. (1985). Negotiations after the sale: the roots and ramifications of conflict in an acquisition. *Journal of Occupational Behaviour*, (6). 65–84.

Nahavandi, A. & Malekzadeh, A. R. (1988) Acculturation in mergers and acquisitions. *Academy of Management Review*, **13**(1), 79–90.

Napier, N. K. (1989) Mergers and acquisitions: human resource issues and outcomes: a review and suggested typology. *Journal of Management Studies*, (26), 3 May.

Porter, M. (1987) From competitive advantage to corporate strategy. *Harvard Business Review*, May/June, 43–49.

Rankine, D. (1991) Britain's buyers dig deeper. *Acquisitions Monthly*, December, 51–52.

Robino, D. & DeMeuse, K. (1985) Corporate mergers and acquisitions: Their impact on HRM. *Personnel Administrator*, **30**(11), 33–44.

Schweiger, D. M. & DeNisi, A. S. (1991) Communication with employees following a merger: a longitudinal field experiment. *Academy of Management Journal*, **34**(1), 110–135.

Schweiger, D. M. & Ivancevich, J. M. (1985) Human resources: the forgotten factor in mergers and acquisitions. *Personal Administrator*, Nov., 47–61.

Schweiger, D. M., Ivancevich, J. M. & Power, F. R. (1987) Executive action for managing human resources before and after acquisition. *Academy of Management Executive*, **2**, 127–138.

Sinetar, M. (1981) Mergers, morale and productivity. *Personnel Journal*, **60**, 863–867.

Unger, H. (1986) The people trauma of major mergers. *Journal of Industrial Management*, (Canada), **10**, 17 April.

Walsh, J. P. (1988) Top management turnover following mergers and acquisitions. *Strategic Management Journal*, **9**, 173–183.

Walter, G. A. (1985) Culture collisions in mergers and acquisitions. In P. J. Frost, L. F. Moore, M. R. Louis, C. C. Lundberg & J. Martin (Eds.) *Organisational Culture*. Beverley Hills: Sage Publications.

Wanous, J. P. (1980) *Organisational Entry: Recruitment, Selection and Socialisation of Newcomers*. Reading, MA: Addison-Wesley.

Young (1981) A conclusive investigation into the causative elements of failure in acquisitions and mergers. In S. J. Lee & R. D. Colman (Eds.) *Handbook of Mergers, Acquisitions & Buyouts*. NJ: Prentice Hall, 605–628.

CHAPTER 5

Work and Family: In Search of More Effective Workplace Interventions

Julian Barling

Queen's University, Kingston, Ontario, Canada

The interdependence of work and family has become an extremely popular subject for study and speculation over the past decade or so, although research on this topic is by no means a recent phenomenon (Barling, 1990, 1992). The earlier research assuming an overlap between work and family roles (e.g. Hoppock, 1935; Mathews, 1934) was followed by contrary suggestions that there was a rigid structural differentiation between work and family roles (Parsons, 1959). Later, Hall (1972) suggested that work and family roles overlapped for women, but not for men.

Currently, there are no challenges to the notion that work influences family functioning. The literature is replete with examples of how (negative) work experiences are associated with (detrimental) influences on family functioning. Organizational scholars and researchers also acknowledge that family functioning influences work, but they have devoted substantially less attention to this notion.

Given the consistency of findings relating work and family, and the social importance of this issue, it is not surprising that numerous interventions have been designed and implemented to enable people, usually women, to be able to balance the needs of work and family more

Trends in Organizational Behavior, Volume 1. Edited by C. L. Cooper and D. M. Rousseau
© 1994 John Wiley & Sons Ltd.

effectively. Certainly, there have been numerous attempts to do just this. To date, most organizational responses to the challenge of helping employees better balance the demands of work and family life have been structural in nature. Perhaps the two most frequent interventions would be flexible shift schedules, and different forms of child care arrangements.

It is important from the perspective of this chapter to examine the implicit assumptions on which such interventions are based. First, interventions designed to rearrange work schedules to be more compatible with family demands would be predicated on the assumption that work only exerts negative effects on the family in the extent to which it keeps people away from their families. Hence, if work can be rearranged (as with flexible work schedules) to allow people to spend more time with their families, employees would be able to better balance the often competing demands of work and family life. Second and somewhat similarly, on-site child care arrangements are based on the assumption that if work can be arranged to allow employees to be closer to other family members, many of the family problems occasioned by work could be overcome.

In this respect, therefore, such interventions find their basis in a "deprivation" framework (Barling, 1990). In the extent to which work takes employees away from their families, work necessarily plays the role of the villain.[1] The longer one is away from the family, the greater the negative effect of the work. The consequences of empirically validating this assumption would be somewhat pessimistic, inasmuch as it is doubtful whether people have the flexibility to reduce the number of hours they work because of the close association between the number of hours worked and pay, and because organizations might not be willing to reduce the number of hours worked by most of their employees.

ALTERNATIVE PERSPECTIVES

A more fundamental and optimistic understanding of the literature linking work and family, however, would suggest that such structural attempts at intervention may not be sufficient to effect an appropriate balance between work and family. This is because the basis underlying these assumptions may not reflect the work–family balance or the needs

---

[1] This is not to say that, in understanding the interdependence of work and family, the family cannot also fulfil the role of villain. It can and under some circumstances does, such as when individuals experiencing a divorce find their work negatively affected (Kriegsmann & Hardin, 1974). However, this is beyond the scope of this chapter.

of employees and families appropriately. An understanding of why this is the case rests on the acceptance of several alternative assumptions, each of which have wide support in the empirical literature (see especially Barling, 1990, 1992).

Assumption 1: The quality of the work, rather than the amount or timing of work, is critical to understanding the balance between work and family.

The earliest research linking work and family was driven by the assumption that the more time a mother or wife devoted to employment, the more she was drawn away from her maternal or spousal duties, which would necessarily exert a negative effect on the family (e.g. Mathews, 1934). This can be seen clearly if the research strategy used most frequently in research investigating the presumed consequences of maternal employment is examined. Most such research simply contrasted employed and non-employed mothers. Some of this research went one step further, focusing specifically on the number of hours worked by mothers (see Barling, 1990, Chapter 7). Reviews over a four decade period have noted that this strategy has failed to yield consistent effects associated with the quantity of employment (Barling, 1990; Bronfenbrenner & Crouter, 1982; Hoffman, 1961, 1986; Stolz, 1960), despite the continuing belief that such effects do exist (Jensen & Borges, 1986). This is illustrated well by Jensen and Borges' (1986) comment after several decades of research searching for any negative effects of maternal employment, that "... the failure to find significant differences between these two groups does not mean that there are no differences" (p.659).

Bronfenbrenner and Crouter (1982) likened this earlier research contrasting employed v. non-employed mothers with a focus on a mother's "daily social address". Together with other commentators (e.g. Barling & Van Bart, 1984; Hoffman, 1986) Bronfenbrenner and Crouter (1982) called for researchers to move beyond this traditional "deprivation" approach that equates employment with a linear metric of time, to focus instead on the *consequences* of the subjective meaning of employment. Our recent research has been guided by such calls, and has yielded results that support the assumption that it is the quality, rather than the timing or amount of work, that helps us understand any effects of work on the family. In addition, these studies also go further in identifying *which* work experiences indirectly affect diverse aspects of family functioning.

Some earlier studies had started to show a significant relationship between mothers' job satisfaction and mother–child interactions (Harrell & Ridley, 1975) and children's behaviours (Barling & Van Bart, 1984).

MacEwen and Barling (1991) took this perspective further, however, by showing how different work experiences, namely role dissatisfaction and work–family conflict, exert different indirect effects on children's behaviours. Specifically, consistent with the initial hypotheses, interrole conflict as a stressor was cognitively and emotionally distracting, and therefore affected both concentration and negative mood respectively. In contrast, role dissatisfaction is not cognitively overloading, and hence only affected negative mood. As will be noted in discussing the assumption that work exerts indirect effects on family functioning, each of these two consequences affects different aspects of parent–child interactions and children's behaviours.

Because it appears as though the effects of work experiences on children's behavior may be gender specific (i.e. mothers' *employment* but fathers' *unemployment* exerts negative effects on children and the marital relationship; see Barling, 1990), it must be noted that fathers' employment experiences exert similar effects on their children. While there is considerably less research and speculation focusing on fathers' work and family well-being, fathers' job satisfaction is associated with positive father–son interactions and their sons' social behaviours, and different working experiences influence parent–child interactions and children's behaviours differently (Barling, 1986a; Stewart & Barling, 1993).

The same pattern holds when the relationship of work experiences and marital functioning is investigated. Work stressors affect one's own marital functioning and marital violence (Barling, 1986b; Barling & Rosenbaum, 1986) as well as one's spouse's marital functioning (MacEwen & Barling, 1993). However, as will become apparent in discussing the second assumption, the indirect effects of work stressors on marital functioning are far more significant than any direct effects.

Three related studies have lent support to our notion that the *quality* of one's role experience is critical to understanding the interdependence of work and family, rather than one's role status. First, we showed that while unemployment *status* is not associated with marital functioning (Grant & Barling, in press), one's experience during unemployment (e.g. time structure) does indirectly predict marital satisfaction and marital aggression. Second, homemakers' role experiences (e.g. level of perceived skill use, role overload, perceived financial equity and satisfaction with the homemaker role) indirectly predict parent–toddler interactions, and toddlers' behaviours (Barling et al, 1993). Lastly, retirement experiences (e.g. time use) also indirectly predicts marital satisfaction (Higginbottom, Barling & Kelloway, 1993).

The findings of these latter three studies are important, because if the general hypothesis about the quality of the work experience is tenable, then the quality of non-employment role experiences should also affect family functioning. In this sense, these three studies certainly provide additional support for this first assumption.

Assumption 2: Work experiences exert indirect effects on family functioning.

Conceptual models (e.g. spillover model; Barling, 1990, 1992) classifying the relationship between job and life satisfaction on the one hand, and marital satisfaction on the other hand, are based on the assumption of a direct link between work and family, an assumption that would not require intervening or mediating variables to fully explain the relationship between work and family. Similarly, research that seeks zero-order correlations between the amount of time spent at work and family functioning, or even the quality of work experiences and family functioning, and interventions that restructure work to allow employees greater access to family members, are based on the same assumption of a direct relationship between work and family.

Beginning with a study on maternal employment experiences (MacEwen & Barling, 1991), our research programme on employment and non-employment roles has now accumulated sufficient data to cast serious doubt on the assumption of a direct relationship between work and family. Instead, we now suggest that, in general, work stressors affect personal well-being (e.g. mood, concentration), well-being in turn affects parent–child interactions, which then influence children's behaviour. In our earlier study (MacEwen & Barling, 1991), we argued that because of their overarousing nature, work stressors would heighten arousal and decrease attention; and therefore interrole conflict should influence cognitive distraction. Consistent with a large body of research, we also maintained that work stressors have a detrimental effect on mood, an affective manifestation of personal well-being. Along the same lines, we argued that role satisfaction would only predict mood, and not cognitive distraction, because dissatisfaction is not overarousing (Figure 5.1). These hypotheses were strongly supported.

From the perspective of the assumption that work experiences exert indirect effects on family functioning, it is important to note that negative mood and cognitive distraction then exerted distinct effects on aspects of family functioning (MacEwen & Barling, 1991). Specifically, mothers who were cognitively distracted were perceived as being rejecting by their children, probably because of an inability by the mothers to concentrate on the issues that were salient to the children. In contrast, negative mood is associated both with rejecting and punishing parenting behaviours. In turn, these different parenting styles

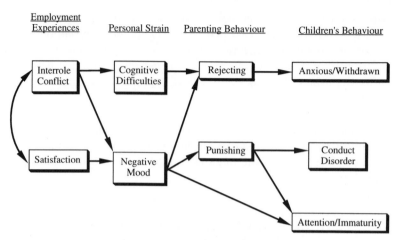

Figure 5.1   Process model linking work experiences and family functioning

differentially predict children's behaviours (conduct disorder, anxious/withdrawn behaviour and attention/immaturity).

We have replicated this general trend in several other studies. For example, fathers' work experiences are indirectly associated with their children's behaviour (Stewart & Barling, 1993), while the relationship between work experiences and marital functioning is mediated by negative mood (or depressive symptoms) and cognitive distraction (Barling & MacEwen, 1992; MacEwen & Barling, 1993). Similarly, eldercare-based interrole conflict indirectly affects marital functioning (Barling et al, in press).

Again extending this focus, non-employment roles such as homemaking (Barling et al, 1993), unemployment (Grant & Barling, in press) and retirement (Higginbottom et al, 1993) are also linked with marital functioning via negative mood. What is also important to note is that in some of these studies (e.g. Barling & MacEwen, 1992; MacEwen & Barling, 1993), the indirect effects of work on family are more salient than the direct effects. Indeed, in some cases there are no direct effects at all (e.g. Barling & MacEwen, 1992) yet there is still strong support for indirect effects of diverse work stressors on marital functioning. Consequently, empirical support is provided for this second assumption.

Assumption 3: The quality of parent–child interactions is more important to children's well-being than the amount of time spent together.

This third assumption is as important in driving the argument presented in this chapter. We will not devote much attention to this third assumption, however, for two primary reasons. First, it lies beyond the realm of organizational behaviour (but for a discussion, see Barling, 1990, especially Chapters 4, and 6–8). Second, and perhaps more importantly, it is widely accepted as self-evident in the fields of clinical, developmental or family psychology.

Suffice it to reiterate, however, that the quality of parent–child interactions is substantially more important to the long-term well-being of the child than mere access to a parent.[2] Obviously, the same argument holds true for spousal interactions and the quality of the spousal relationship.

TOWARD MORE EFFECTIVE ORGANIZATIONAL INTERVENTIONS

To reiterate, the majority of interventions currently invoked to help employees balance the often competing needs of work and family have invariably been focused on the notion of restructuring work to give employees more time with their families, or greater access to their children during work (e.g. through on-site child care). As already noted, this strategy is based on the assumption that work is detrimental to the family in the extent to which it keeps employees away from their families.

The results of the studies presented above, and the arguments put forward against the current assumptions, do not necessarily mean that strategies or interventions such as on-site day care are ineffectual. Instead, they suggest that such strategies by themselves will not be sufficient to effect long-term and meaningful changes. The rationale for this argument is derived from the fourth major assumption, namely:

Assumption 4: It will avail little to restructure work to ensure more contact between family members if work experiences are sufficiently negative to lead to negative affect and negative interactions, and thereby exert a negative and indirect effect on family functioning.

Over-and-above any interventions designed to increase the time family members spend with each other, therefore, what is required is an attempt to ensure that work enhances personal well-being. Certainly, when children come into contact with their parents, research findings

---

[2] Of course this does not imply that access is unimportant—rather it is a necessary but insufficient factor in understanding the effects of parent–child interactions.

suggest that children as young as eight years old are aware of what their parents do at work, *and* how they feel about their jobs (Abramovitch & Johnson, 1992; Hamper, 1991). Thus, if the findings from our research (e.g. Barling & MacEwen, 1992; MacEwen & Barling, 1991, 1993; MacEwen, Barling & Kelloway, 1992) can be used as a guide, work that enhances positive mood and personal satisfaction will be most likely to lead to positive interactions between family members, and parenthetically will also lead to young children holding positive views about the world of work in general. As Piotrkowski and Stark (1987, p.7) note: "As they listen to their parents talk about their jobs, as they see their parents come home tired after a hard day at work, as they spend time at parents' workplaces, they may develop feelings and ideas about work."

Recent research on job redesign shows that changes in work-related psychological well-being can be achieved with minimal changes in job design, and this enables an optimistic perspective about the possibilities of designing interventions to balance work and family demands more effectively. One example of a field study on job design in which careful assessment of mental health and productivity effects took place will suffice here. Wall et al (1990) studied a situation that was characteristic of specialist control and therefore low in autonomy. Operators loaded, monitored and unloaded machines in an advanced manufacturing technology environment, and when operating problems arose, they were obliged to call on a specialist (identified by the organization) to correct the problem. The job was then redesigned by the workers and one of the authors of the study to be more consistent with an operator-controlled system, in which the operators became more responsible for correcting operating problems at their source without recourse to the "expert". Consistent with this, the design of the job changed from one in which little autonomy was offered, to one that afforded the employee greater autonomy, skill variety, task identity and task significance, the hallmarks of a well-designed job (Hackman & Oldham, 1980).

The effects of the change on psychological well-being were certainly noteworthy. There were statistically significant increases in intrinsic job satisfaction and decreases in job pressure as the design of the job changed from specialist to operator control. What is also important is that these changes occurred at the same time as there were clear increases in productivity, despite the fact that there were no pay or any other extrinsic job changes. This suggests strongly that relatively modest and inexpensive changes in job design can lead to positive changes in psychological well-being on the job, which we assume will promote more positive family interactions.

But the question still remains: Do such changes in the job environment necessarily spill over into the home? Aside from empirical findings over a few decades showing positive correlations between job satisfaction and marital satisfaction (e.g. Barling & Rosenbaum, 1986; Dyer, 1956; Haavio-Mannila, 1971), Crouter (1984) reports on a qualitative study which suggests that this carry-over effect does indeed take place. She conducted interviews with 55 blue-collar and supervisory personnel which showed how access to a work environment that provided participation in decision-making led to enhanced family functioning and greater effectiveness as a spouse and parent. As one employee in her study stated: "Working here takes more time away from my personal and family life, but it has helped in terms of dealing with my family. I'm more willing to get their opinions. We hold 'team meetings' at home to make decisions." (Crouter, 1984, p. 82.) This suggests that while employees were aware of the greater time demands placed on them by more "participatory" work, the benefits in terms of interactions within the family were equally visible.

It seems, therefore, that it is possible to design work that enhances well-being, and that some changes may lead directly to improvements in family functioning.

CONCLUSION

To conclude, the traditional framework within which the link between work and family is understood was discussed initially in this chapter, after which a series of alternative assumptions about the effects of work on family were presented. If the reasoning behind these alternative assumptions is accepted, it would follow that the customary ways of trying to balance the needs of work and family would be incomplete. Instead, it was argued that what is required is a combination of the structural changes (e.g. flexible work schedules) with attempts to redesign jobs so that employees' psychological well-being is enhanced by their work. In attempting to alleviate any negative effects of work on the family, interventions that focus on job design should be encouraged, and their effectiveness should be evaluated empirically with the scrutiny given to other interventions (e.g. Wall et al, 1990).

AUTHOR NOTES

Preparation of this chapter was facilitated by financial assistance from the Social Sciences and Humanities Research Council of Canada.

Reprints may be obtained from Dr Julian Barling, School of Business, Queen's University, Kingston, Ontario K7L 3N6.

REFERENCES

Abramovitch, R. & Johnson, L. C. (1992) Children's perceptions of parental work. *Canadian Journal of Behavioural Science*, **24**, 319–332.

Barling, J. (1986a) Fathers' work experiences, the father–child relationship, and children's behaviour. *Journal of Occupational Behaviour*, **7**, 61–66.

Barling, J. (1986b) Interrole conflict and marital functioning amongst employed fathers. *Journal of Occupational Behaviour*, **7**, 1–8.

Barling, J. (1990) *Employment, Stress and Family Functioning*. Chichester: Wiley.

Barling, J. (1992) Work and Family: In Search of the Missing Links. *Journal of Employee Assistance Research*, **1**, 271–285.

Barling, J. & MacEwen, K. E. (1992) Linking work experiences and marital functioning. *Journal of Organizational Behaviour*, **13**, 573–583.

Barling, J. & Rosenbaum, A. (1986) Work stressors and wife abuse. *Journal of Applied Psychology*, **71**, 346–348.

Barling, J. & Van Bart, D. (1984) Mothers' subjective employment experiences and the behaviours of their nursery school children. *Journal of Occupational Psychology*, **57**, 49–56.

Barling, J., MacEwen, K. E., Kelloway, E. K. & Higginbottom, S. F. (in press) Predictors and outcomes of eldercare-based interrole conflict. *Psychology and Aging*.

Barling, J., MacEwen, K. E. & Nolte, M. L. (1993) Homemaker role experiences influence toddler behavior via maternal well-being and parenting behavior. *Journal of Abnormal Child Psychology*, **21**, 213–229.

Bronfenbrenner, U. & Crouter, A. C. (1982) Work and family through time and space. In S. B. Kamerman & C. D. Hayes (Eds.) *Families that Work: Children in a Changing World*. Washington, DC: National Academy Press, pp. 39–83.

Crouter, A. C. (1984) Participative work as an influence on human development. *Journal of Applied Developmental Psychology*, **5**, 71–90.

Dyer, W. G. (1956) A comparison of families of high and low job satisfaction. *Marriage and Family Living*, **18**, 58–60.

Grant, S. & Barling, J. (in press) Linking unemployment experiences, depressive symptoms and marital functioning: A mediational model. In S. L. Sauter et al (Eds.) *Work Stress 2000*. Washington, DC: American Psychological Association.

Haavio-Mannila, E. (1971) Satisfaction with family, work, leisure and life among men and women. *Human Relations*, **24**, 585–601.

Hackman, R. J. & Oldham, G. R. (1980) *Work Redesign*. Reading, MA: Addison-Wesley.

Hall, D. T. (1972) A model of coping with role conflict. *Adminstrative Science Quarterly*, **4**, 471–486.

Hamper, B. (1991) *Rivethead: Tales from the Assembly Line*. New York: Warner Books.

Harrell, J. E. & Ridley, C. A. (1975) Substitute child care, maternal employment and the quality of mother–child interactions. *Journal of Marriage and the Family*, **37**, 556–564.

Higginbottom, S. F., Barling, J. & Kelloway, E. K. (1993) Linking retirement experiences and marital satisfaction: A mediational model. *Psychology and Aging*, **8**, 508–516.

Hoffman, L. W. (1961) Effects of maternal employment on the child. *Child Development*, **32**, 187–197.

Hoffman, L. W. (1986) Work, family and the child. In M. S. Pollock & R. O.

Perloff (Eds.) *Psychology and work: Productivity, change and employment.* Washington, DC: American Psychological Association, pp.173–220.

Hoppock, R. (1935) *Job Satisfaction.* New York: Harper & Row.

Jensen, L. & Borges, M. (1986) The effect of maternal employment on adolescent daughters. *Adolescence,* **21,** 659–666.

Kriegsmann, J. K. & Hardin, D. R. (1974) Does divorce hamper job performance? *The Personnel Administrator,* **19,** 26–29.

MacEwen, K. E. & Barling, J. (1991) Effects of maternal employment experiences on children's behavior mood, cognitive difficulties, and parenting behavior. *Journal of Marriage and the Family,* **53,** 635–644.

MacEwen, K. E. & Barling, J. (1993) Type A behavior and marital satisfaction: Differential effects of achievement striving and impatience/irritability. *Journal of Marriage and the Family,* **55,** 1001–1010.

MacEwen, K. E., Barling, J. & Kelloway, E. K. (1992) Effects of short-term role overload on marital interactions. *Work and Stress,* **6,** 117–126.

Mathews, S. M. (1934) The effects of mothers' out of home employment upon their children's ideas and attitudes. *Journal of Applied Psychology,* **19,** 116–136.

Parsons, T. (1959) The social structure of the family. In R. N. Emshen (Ed.) *The Family: Its Function and Destiny.* New York: Harper & Row, pp.241–274.

Piotrkowski, C. S. & Stark, E. (1987) Children and adolescents look at their parents' jobs. In J. H. Lewko (Ed.) *How Children and Adolescents View the World of Work* San Francisco, CA: Jossey-Bass, pp.3–19.

Stewart, W. & Barling, J. (1993) Fathers' work experiences and their children's social behaviours and school competencies. Manuscript in preparation, Department of Psychology, Queen's University, Kingston, Ontario K7L 3N6.

Stolz, L. M. (1960) Effects of maternal employment on children: Evidence from research. *Child Development,* **31,** 749–763.

Wall, T. D., Corbett, J. M., Martin, R., Clegg, C. W. & Jackson, P. R. (1990) Advanced manufacturing technology, work design, and performance: A change study. *Journal of Applied Psychology,* **75,** 691–697.

CHAPTER 6

Personality and Personnel Selection

Ivan T. Robertson

University of Manchester, Institute of Science and Technology, UK

Personality constructs and theoretical ideas from the personality domain have featured in the personnel selection research literature in only a limited number of ways. By far the most important and extensively researched theme involves the use of personality assessment in personnel selection decision-making. This chapter concentrates on this use of personality assessment.

Most psychologists divide human individual differences into two broad categories: intelligence (general mental ability) and personality. There is considerable evidence that scores on tests of general mental ability are closely linked to success in a wide variety of occupational areas (Hunter & Hunter, 1984). Some practitioners and researchers seem reluctant to accept and act on this finding. Certainly the use of ability testing is far less widespread than research evidence alone would lead one to expect. The use of such tests is complicated by various issues such as the relatively poor scores obtained by some subgroups of the population and the restricted range of scores obtained for some applicant groups (e.g. university graduates); nevertheless the scientific evidence is clear.

The position with personality assessment is rather different and if anything, the use of personality assessment procedures in organizations has been far more widespread than research evidence would support. It seems that many human resource practitioners feel that personality factors have an important role to play in determining job success. Hard,

Trends in Organizational Behavior, Volume 1. Edited by C. L. Cooper and D. M. Rousseau
© 1994 John Wiley & Sons Ltd.

scientific evidence to support all of the uses to which personality measures are put is not available. As this chapter will show there is, however, evidence that personality characteristics are important in determining work behaviour and that there is a role for personality assessment in personnel selection. Personality assessment procedures are prominent in organizations and are used in selection decisions, placement and career development. By contrast with intelligence testing the research evidence to support the use of personality assessment has emerged only recently and is still much less extensive.

APPROACHES TO PERSONALITY

There is no single unifying theory of personality within psychology. Psychologists share an understanding that personality concerns the factors of temperament and disposition that are responsible for some of the differences between people and the cross-situational similarities in any individual's behaviour. Mischel (1993) identified five major approaches to personality: psychodynamic; trait and biological; phenomenological; behavioural and cognitive–social. One major way in which these approaches to personality differ is the extent to which they emphasize the role of external (situational) forces or that of stable psychological (person) forces. Early behavioural approaches stressed the role of the reinforcing or punishing aspects of the situation and placed little emphasis on internal, psychological factors. By contrast, psychodynamic approaches focus on the role of internal, often unconscious, psychological forces. Phenomenological approaches stress that the meaning of events is different for each individual and also focus attention on within-person factors. Another major way in which personality theories differ concerns the extent to which they provide procedures for measuring individual differences so that personalities of individuals may be examined and the personalities of different people compared. Although cognitive–social approaches incorporate roles for person and situational factors there is no unique system for personality measurement associated with this approach. Trait approaches to personality provide a set of dimensions that may be used to describe the characteristics of individuals. The associated tests and questionnaires that have been developed may be used to provide profiles of the personalities of different people and to make comparisons between them on a one to one basis or, with the aid of extensive normative data, to compare individuals with a relevant population or subgroup. The capability of trait/factor analytic approaches to measure, compare, classify and evaluate people has made them popular amongst personnel psychologists and human resource practitioners. Other theoretical views of human personality may have the potential to contribute to personnel selection decision-making but so far this potential, if it exists, has not been realized.

PERSONALITY IN CONTEXT

In recent years scholars in the organization behaviour field have debated the primacy of dispositional or situational factors in the determination of people's outlook and behaviour. On the one side interesting and important research, exemplified by the controversial article of Staw and Ross (1985), suggests that even qualities such as job satisfaction, which by definition seem to be situationally determined, may have a stable dispositional component. Staw and Ross (1985) found correlations of 0.24 for job satisfaction measures taken five years apart (1966–1971) for a sample of men who had changed both occupation and employer during the period. This compared with a correlation of 0.37 for men who had stayed in the same occupation with the same employer. Although subsequent research (Newton & Keenen, 1991) has questioned the methodology used by Staw and Ross (1985) it has also reinforced the finding that job and work attitudes show stability even when situations change. Another, related line of research has offered support for the view that job and work attitudes and values may have a genetic component. Most of this work has involved kinship studies in which the scores of individuals of varying genetic and environmental similarity (e.g. identical twins reared apart) are compared. In the first study of its kind focusing on job satisfaction Arvey et al (1989) found an intraclass correlation coefficient of 0.31 for the general job satisfaction scores of a set of identical twins reared apart. Clearly it is unlikely that job satisfaction is inherited directly. It may be, however, as Arvey et al (1989) theorize, that some stable personality characteristics are partly genetically determined and in turn influence job satisfaction scores. For example, if the tendency to construe events in a negative way (known as negative affect, Watson & Clark, 1984) is partly inherited this tendency would spill over into evaluations of various features of a person's life, including satisfaction with a job. In fact there is clear evidence to show that both negative affect and positive affect (Watson & Clark, 1984) exert some influence on a variety of variables, such as job satisfaction, that might, at face value, seem to be entirely situationally determined. Positive affect is not merely the antithesis of negative affect but refers to a distinct personality dimension that is independent of negative affectivity.

> Positive affect reflects the extent to which a person is feeling a zest for life, feeling up versus down. High positive affect is most clearly defined by

words such as active, excited, alert, enthusiastic and strong, whereas low positive affect is best characterized by terms reflecting fatigue such as sluggish and drowsy. Negative affect, in contrast, represents the extent to which a person feels upset or unpleasantly aroused versus peaceful. High negative affect includes a wide variety of unpleasant states (e.g. distressed, nervous, angry, guilty and scornful), whereas low negative affect is marked by terms such as calm and relaxed. (Watson & Clark, 1984; p. 472).

Using alternative terminology negative affect is emotional stability or neuroticism and positive affect is extraversion (Eysenck, 1970). If dispositional characteristics such as positive and negative affect exert a pervasive influence this would be expected to show in both work and non-work areas of an individual's life. Research has indeed revealed links between work and non-work well-being (Warr, 1990). Research evidence has also shown that job satisfaction is related to measures of negative and positive affect in ways that would be expected (see Furnham & Zacherl, 1986; Levin & Stokes, 1989). This research offers convincing support for the pervasive influence of personality factors.

Research evidence in favour of situational effects is also compelling. A long and successful stream of work, based originally on the behavioural framework developed by Skinner and others (Luthans & Martinko, 1987), has shown that the manipulation of reinforcing and punishing features of the environment can exert a powerful influence on behaviour. Experiments involving the design of work to incorporate the job characteristics of skill variety, task identity, task significance, autonomy and feedback (Fried & Ferris, 1987) have revealed that changes in behaviour and outlook can be brought about.

An impartial reading of the available research leads to the inescapable conclusion that both situations and disposition are involved in the determination of behaviour. Bandura (1986) has provided the framework of "reciprocal determinism" to illustrate the joint interacting effects of person (dispositional) and situational variables with behaviour (Figure 6.1).

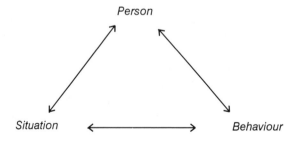

Figure 6.1   Reciprocal determinism

In this framework behaviour is a function of both person and situational variables. In turn behaviour may exert an influence on situational and personal factors. For example, although a strong situation may exert a major influence on behaviour, it is also possible for a person to behave in a way that changes the situation. When this framework is applied to the elements involved in personnel selection it becomes very clear that it is impossible to predict anyone's future work behaviour from a knowledge of his or her personal qualities only. Although knowledge of the person (e.g. personality characteristics and mental ability) might provide a basis for partial understanding of future behaviour a knowledge of the situation is also important in providing a complete picture. This analysis shows quite clearly that there is likely to be a ceiling, determined by the extent to which situational factors have been taken into account, to the accuracy of any personnel selection method.

As yet there is no universal procedure for incorporating knowledge of situational factors into personnel selection processes. Many factors might be involved in determining the role of situational factors but at least two seem to be of particular importance when personality assessment is considered.

Job analysis is an often recommended first stage in the personnel selection process. Although most personnel selection texts do not highlight the fact, conducting a job analysis represents a systematic way of paying attention to some of the situational factors that may be important in determining a job holder's performance. Job analysis also provides a basis for drawing inferences about which personality characteristics or other psychological variables may be important for job success. It would be reasonable to expect that validity studies involving personality constructs would produce more positive results when the selection of personality constructs measured has been based on systematic job analysis.

Job Performance Criteria

The second important factor is the nature of the job performance criteria used. It is well recognized in the personnel selection literature that some performance criteria are more prone to contamination than others. Often this contamination is the result of situational factors. Raw sales figures, for example, reflect the performance of the salesperson and the area in which he or she works. This suggests that some criteria are likely to be more situationally dependent than others and thus less predictable from a knowledge of an individual's personal make-up. As noted earlier this impact of the situation is usually treated as contamination or error in the criterion measurement. At a more general level it reflects a need to incorporate some influence for situational variables in personnel selection research. The specificity of the criteria used is also an important issue. Successful overall job performance may be attained with a variety of different personality profiles; for example extroversion may be an asset only if combined with agreeableness. For most other selection procedures the scores for the component measures involved would be expected to combine positively to enhance overall job performance. High performance on all of the exercises in an assessment centre would be a much stronger signal of good job performance than some combination of high and low performance. For personality constructs the position is more complex. The theoretical sophistication of models linking personality constructs to job performance is not yet sufficient to provide clear predictions of how personal factors might combine to enhance or diminish overall performance. It is, however, realistic to make predictions, based on theory, about the links between personality constructs and specific job competences. This suggests that studies using personality constructs should not focus only on overall job performance but also at the more specific level of particular job competences.

CRITERION-RELATED VALIDITY

Since the late 1970s researchers' views of the validity of personnel selection methods have undergone significant change. Before this period the consensus view was that the validity of methods was inconsistent and generally rather meagre. What researchers had failed to take account of was that most validity studies were conducted on small samples, often with a restricted range of scores and unreliable measuring procedures. When corrections were made for these artefacts, with the aid of meta-analysis procedures (Hunter & Schmidt, 1990), the conclusion that validities for most methods were inconsistent and poor was shown to be false. Throughout the 1980s a series of meta-analyses were conducted to evaluate more accurately the validity of all of the major personnel selection procedures. Encouraging validity coefficients were found for many personnel selection procedures. Assessment centres (Gaugler et al, 1987), structured, job-related interviews (Wiesner & Cronshaw, 1988), work sample tests (Hunter & Hunter, 1984; Robertson & Downs, 1989) and mental ability tests (Schmitt et al, 1984) were all found to display good levels of criterion-related validity.

Personality Constructs Used in Personnel Selection

Historically a large number of different personality constructs have been utilized in personnel selection research. Often the constructs used have been drawn from general personality instruments, which measure a range of traits, such as the Sixteen PF (Cattell, Eber & Tatsuoka, 1970), the California Personality Inventory (Gough, 1987), the Minnesota Multiphasic Personality Inventory (Hathaway & McKinley, 1943) etc. More specific personality constructs such as locus of control (Rotter, 1966) or type A behaviour pattern (Friedman & Rosenman, 1974) have also been investigated. Until recently there were few generalizable findings and the prevailing climate of opinion amongst researchers was in line with the view expressed by Guion and Gottier (1965) that there was no evidential basis for recommending the use of personality testing in selection situations. Part of the difficulty in evaluating findings and organizing research into the criterion-related validity of personality constructs lay in the lack of a clear consensus concerning the nature of the major personality dimensions. For many years Eysenck (e.g. Eysenck, 1970; Eysenck & Eysenck, 1985) presented evidence and argued that two of the fundamental dimensions of personality were emotional stability and extraversion. More recent work has confirmed this view and added three other key dimensions to the personality psychologists' lexicon: conscientiousness; agreeableness and openness to experience. Low and high scorers on these characteristics are described below (from Costa & McCrae, 1985).

- Openness: high scorers are open to new experiences, have broad interests and are very imaginative; low scorers are down-to-earth, practical, traditional and pretty much set in their ways.
- Agreeableness: high scorers are compassionate, good-natured, and eager to cooperate and avoid conflict; low scorers are hardheaded, sceptical, proud and competitive. They tend to express anger directly.
- Conscientiousness: high scorers are conscientious and well-organized, have high standards and always strive to achieve goals; low scorers are easygoing, not very well-organized and sometimes careless. They prefer not to make plans.

Together with extraversion and emotional stability (mentioned earlier in this chapter) these factors make up the so-called "big five" personality characteristics. The big five factors have been confirmed when using various data collection procedures and in several different languages, including English, Dutch, German and Japanese (John, 1990). They have also been shown to be stable over time (McCrae and Costa, 1990). Much of the more recent research on the criterion-related validity of personality has used the big five as an organizing framework or has focused on specific job-relevant factors such as integrity (see Ones, Viswesvaran & Schmidt, 1993) or service orientation (Hogan, Hogan & Busch, 1984).

The Criterion-Related Validity of Personality Assessment

An early attempt to provide a quantifiable indication of the criterion-related validity of personality was reported by Ghiselli and Barthol (1953). Although some useful validities were found, Ghiselli and Barthol were not encouraging about the use of personality instruments in personnel selection. The first meta-analysis using the Schmidt–Hunter (Hunter & Schmidt, 1990) procedures to provide evidence on the criterion-related validity of personality assessment (Schmidt et al, 1984) found an overall validity of only 0.15 (uncorrected for unreliability or range restriction).

Although the initial meta-analysis results for personality assessment were not encouraging there are good reasons to believe that the results obtained were underestimating the validity of personality constructs. These reasons are discussed more fully in Robertson (1993). Briefly, the meta-analytic procedures used to estimate the criterion-related validity of personality constructs need to be different from those used for other personnel selection methods. The essence of the difference is that hypothesis-driven procedures need to be used when personality constructs are being evaluated. With other personnel selection methods clear hypotheses are nearly always explicitly or implicitly used in the individual studies that are subjected to meta-analysis. For example the components of a work sample test will have been derived from job analysis and the scores produced on all aspects of the test will be expected to correlate with job performance. When personality measures are used in a validity study it is common for all of the dimensions measured by a particular test to be included, even when there is no strong expectation that every dimension will be linked with job performance. The averaging process used in meta-analysis to estimate criterion-related validity for a set of local validation studies on personality needs to ensure that only personality dimensions that are expected to relate to the criteria are included. More recent meta-analysis (e.g. Barrick & Mount, 1991; Tett, Jackson & Rothstein, 1991) have shown that when hypothesis driven procedures are used better results are obtained. The clearest demonstration of this is provided in some of the results obtained by Tett et al (1991). When a global averaging of all of the coefficients from the studies examined by Tett et al (1991) was conducted the resulting estimate of the population validity (0.16) was very close to that obtained by Schmitt et al (1984) using similar procedures (0.15). When Tett et al (1991) focused on studies in which confirmatory research strategies and job analysis had been used to select personality constructs the results were much better. For these studies the mean sample size-weighted validity coefficient was 0.25 (0.38 when corrected for unreliability), though it should be noted that there were only seven studies in this category.

A study conducted by Robertson and Kinder (1993) examined links between personality constructs and specific competences using an hypothesis driven procedure. Robertson and Kinder used practitioners who were trained in the use of a specific personality instrument (the Occupational Personality Questionnaire (OPQ); Saville & Holdsworth, 1990) to generate hypotheses linking personality constructs with job competences. Meta-analytic procedures were then used to cumulate the results from a sample of studies to investigate the hypothesized relationships. The resulting mean sample-size weighted validity coefficients (uncorrected for unreliability or restriction of range) varied from 0.09 to 0.33. Robertson and Kinder also examined the extent to which personality variables provided incremental validity beyond that provided by measures of mental ability. Their results revealed very little overlap between the criterion variance correlated with ability and that associated with personality, suggesting that personality constructs provide unique information about potential performance at work. Further support for this conclusion has been given by Barrick, Mount and Strauss (1993) who also found that personality and ability variables contributed non-overlapping variance associated with performance measures.

As far as specific job-relevant scales are concerned good validities have been obtained for both integrity testing (Ones et al, 1993) and service orientation (Hogan et al, 1984).

It is worth noting that the studies mentioned above have focused on personality characteristics at fairly high levels of generality (the big five) and at more detailed levels of analysis. The criteria used have also varied in level, with some studies focusing on overall work performance and others concentrating on more specific criteria such as particular job competences. Both levels of analysis seem to be important in obtaining a better understanding of the role of personality in work performance. Obviously it is important to examine the extent to which overall performance may be dependent on personality. In reality though the links between overall performance and personality are likely to be mediated by specific competences. A conceptual framework linking personality to work performance thus needs to include several elements: personality constructs; work competences; situational variables; job demands; overall work performance and for completeness, genetic and environmental determinants of personality. Figure 6.2 illustrates this framework.

As the evidence reviewed briefly above reveals, personality is a function of both environmental and genetic factors. In turn, according to

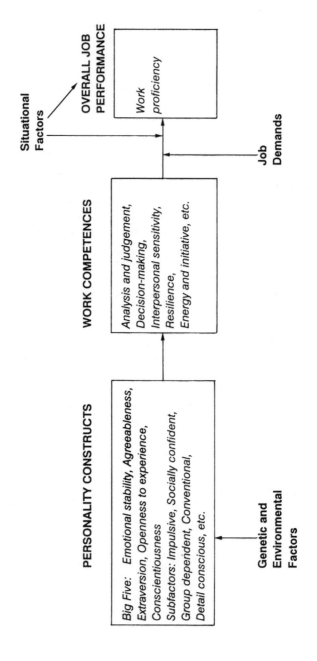

Figure 6.2 Personality and job performance

the framework in Figure 6.2, personality factors help to determine work competences. Depending upon the job demands and the work situation these competences then combine and interact to influence overall performance. The demands of the job determine the relative importance of each competence to overall performance. The specific competences act as mediators between the underlying personality variables and overall effectiveness. Barrick, Mount and Strauss (1993), for example, have shown how the setting of goals mediates the links between conscientiousness and overall job performance. To give substance to Figure 6.2, the big five personality characteristics have been included as personality factors and illustrative competences from those employed by Robertson and Kinder (1993) have been used. It is important to stress, however, that although there is some consensus amongst personality researchers on the big five, there is no such consensus on a set of generic work competences. Indeed, as work on the measurement of such variables using assessment centre technology suggests (e.g. Bycio, Alvares & Hahn, 1987) there is considerable uncertainty about the extent to which discrete competences can be identified and measured. The influence of situational variables is also awkward to deal with. Again there is no commonly agreed framework or set of variables to use. Recent work is, however, beginning to provide some clarification of the role that situational variables can play. Barrick and Mount (1993) have shown that, for jobs that are high in autonomy, the links between personality constructs and performance are stronger than they are for lower autonomy jobs. This is very much in line with the more general theoretical proposition that individual difference variables, such as personality, will exert more influence when situations are weak and will be less important in strong, highly constraining settings (Adler & Weiss, 1988).

AN AGENDA FOR FUTURE WORK

The results presented above show that there is a useful role for personality testing to play in personnel selection and Figure 6.2 gives a simple framework for looking at personality–performance links. When the personality constructs involved are clear and thought is given to the expected link between these constructs and work behaviour, it is likely that worthwhile information may be derived from personality measurement. In the last decade or so researchers have established links between criterion measures of work behaviour and personality constructs drawn from the big five. Links with criterion measures and personality constructs measured at a more detailed level than the big five have also been established. This information is helpful and has definite applied value but there is some way to go before the research base provides evidence to support the wide-ranging use of personality measurement. This lack of knowledge constrains the extent to which personality testing may be able to contribute to selection and other human resource decisions, such as team building. Everyday experience suggests that the effectiveness of individuals, teams and other organizational units is dependent, in part, upon the personality characteristics of the individuals involved. Research into personality and work performance supports this view and has uncovered linear relationships between various, specific personality constructs and indicators of either overall work performance or specific work-related competences. Unfortunately neither the problems of individual selection nor those of building successful work groups can be resolved with the aid of this knowledge.

First consider the selection of individuals. With the restricted number of personality traits measured in the big five framework there are still many different combinations that might occur in any individual profile. Even if a person's position on each individual characteristic is restricted to high, medium or low 125 ($5 \times 5 \times 5$) possible combinations are possible. If standard ten (sten) scores are used then nearly ten million combinations are possible. If personality is measured using a more detailed level of analysis the possible personality profiles become bewilderingly large (e.g. the 16 personality factors of the 16PF would give over a thousand billion different profiles). It is likely that different personality profiles can lead to equally effective work behaviour and performance since a person's behaviour pattern is a function of how his or her specific personality traits combine to help to determine behaviour in a particular setting. This suggests that for any given job several different combinations of personality characteristics may be effective. All of the recent research mentioned earlier in this chapter is limited to findings about the links between single characteristics and work behaviour. Further progress will be made if investigators begin to address the role of combinations of personality constructs in the determination of behaviour. The problems involved in this kind of research are certainly difficult but may not be as overwhelming as they appear at first sight. Although many different personality profiles exist in principle not all combinations occur in practice; furthermore strong theoretical ideas can be used to limit the personality constructs and interactions of these constructs that will be relevant in any particular setting. There is also some potential in the development of expert system heuristics that are driven by theoretical ideas about how personality constructs combine and interact. In other words it is not necessary to explore the effect of every possible personality mix before being in a position to generate clear guidance, based on evidence. Such systems use theories to build predictions about the behaviour of people with specific profiles and it should be possible to validate the system (i.e. the theory) without the need to examine the behaviour derived from every possible personality profile.

In addition to the need to understand the combined effect of personality characteristics there is the need to understand the shape of the relationship between personality factors and aspects of work behaviour. For example there are work settings where an outgoing person will be more effective than someone who is more reserved (i.e. extroversion will be correlated with work success). It is nevertheless quite easy to imagine that someone who is at the extreme of the extroversion range, particularly if this is coupled with an extreme score on some other factor such as agreeableness, would be less effective than if he or she was less extreme. There is clear evidence that personality characteristics are sometimes related to behaviour in non-linear ways (e.g. Mueller, 1992), though this work is more or less exclusively confined to laboratory studies. Research designed to explore the role of personality in work behaviour, which recognizes and explores non-linear relationships, has the potential to make a significant contribution to both theory and practice.

The performance of anyone who is selected for a position in an organization is likely to be influenced, to some extent, by the situation that he or she works in. For many people the most salient features of the work situation are other people working in the same organization; these may be colleagues, subordinates, bosses or other team members. As shown above, there is considerable complexity in attempting to grasp the role of several personality constructs in relation to the behaviour of one person. Attempting to do this for the behaviour of people who interact at work is an even more challenging task. Relatively little is available in the scientific literature to assist with this task. There are some conceptual frameworks in existence but although these have found favour with some practitioners the scientific evaluation is generally not available or not supportive. Scientifically valid frameworks that help to explain and predict the behaviour of interacting personalities in particular settings would make a major contribution to knowledge and have a very important role to play in practical problem solving and human resource decision-making.

REFERENCES

Adler, S. & Weiss, H. M. (1988) Recent developments in the study of personality and organizational behavior. In C. L. Cooper & I. T. Robertson (Eds.) *International Review of Industrial and Organizational Psychology, 1988*. Chichester: John Wiley.

Arvey, R. D., Bouchard, T. J., Segal, N. L. & Abraham, L. M. (1989) Job satisfaction: Environmental and genetic components. *Journal of Applied Psychology*, **74**, 187–192.

Bandura, A. (1986) *Social Foundations of Thought and Action: A Social Cognitive Theory.* Englewood Cliffs, NJ: Prentice Hall.

Barrick, M. R. & Mount, M. K. (1991) The big five personality dimensions and job performance: A meta-analysis. *Personnel Psychology*, **44**, 1–26.

Barrick, M. R. & Mount, M. K. (1993) Autonomy as a moderator of the relationship between the big five personality dimensions and job performance. *Journal of Applied Psychology*, **78**, 111–118.

Barick, M. R., Mount, M. K. & Strauss, J. P. (1993) Conscientiousness and performance of sales representatives: Test of the mediating effects of goal setting. *Journal of Applied Psychology*, **78**, 715–722.

Bycio, P., Alvares, K. M. & Hahn, J. (1987) Situational specificity in assessment center ratings: A confirmatory factor analysis. *Journal of Applied Psychology*, **72**, 463–474.

Cattell, R. B., Eber, H. W. & Tatsuoka, M. M. (1970) *Handbook for the Sixteen Personality Factor Questionnaire (16PF).* Windsor: National Foundation for Educational Research.

Costa, P. T. & McCrae, R. R. (1985) *Manual for the NEO Personality Inventory.* Odessa, Florida: Psychological Assessment Resources.

Eysenck, H. J. (1970) *The Structure of Human Personality.* London: Methuen.

Eysenck, H. J. & Eysenck, M. J. (1985) *Personality and Individual Differences: A Natural Science Approach.* New York: Plenum Press.

Fried, Y. & Ferris, G. R. (1987) The validity of the job characteristics model: A review and meta-analysis. *Personnel Psychology*, **40**, 287–322.

Friedman, M. D. & Rosenman, R. H. (1974) *Type A Behavior and Your Heart.* New York: Knopf.

Furnham, A. & Zacherl, M. (1986) Personality and job satisfaction. *Personality and Individual Differences*, **7**, 453–459.

Gaugler, B., Rosenthal, D. B., Thornton, G. C. and Bentson, C. (1987) Meta-analysis of assessment center validity. *Journal of Applied Psychology*, **72**, 493–511.

Ghiselli, E. E. & Barthol, R. P. (1953) The validity of personality inventories in the selection of employees. *Journal of Applied Psychology*, **37**, 18–20.

Gough, H. G. (1987) *Manual: The California Psychological Inventory.* Palo Alto, CA: Consulting Psychologists Press.

Guion, R. M. & Gottier, R. F. (1965) Validity of personality measures in personnel selection. *Personnel Psychology*, **18**, 135–164.

Hathaway, S. R. & McKinley, J. C. (1943) *Manual for the Minnesota Multiphasic Personality Inventory.* New York: Psychological Corporation.

Hogan, J., Hogan, R. & Busch, C. M. (1984) How to measure service orientation. *Journal of Applied Psychology*, **69**, 167–173.

Hunter, J. E. & Hunter, R. F. (1984) Validity and utility of alternative predictors of job performance. *Psychological Bulletin*, **96**, 72–98.

Hunter, J. E. & Schmidt, F. L. (1990) *Methods of Meta-Analysis.* Newbury Park: Sage.

John, O. P. (1990) The big five factor taxonomy: Dimensions of personality in natural language and in questionnaires. In L. A. Pervin (Ed.) *Handbook of Personality Theory and Research.* New York: Guilford Press.

Levin, I. & Stokes, J. P. (1989) Dispositional approach to job satisfaction: Role of negative affectivity. *Journal of Applied Psychology*, **74**, 752–758.

Luthans, F. & Martinko, M. (1987) Behavioral approaches to organizations. In C. L. Cooper & I. T. Robertson (Eds.) *International Review of Industrial and Organizational Psychology, 1987.* Chichester: John Wiley.

McCrae, R. R. & Costa, P. T. (1990) *Personality in Adulthood*. New York: Guilford.

Mischel, W. (1993) *Introduction to Personality*, 5th Edition. New York: Holt-Saunders.

Mueller, J. H. (1992) Anxiety and performance. In A. P. Smith & D. M. Jones (Eds.) *Handbook of Human Performance, Volume 3: State and Trait*. London: Academic Press.

Newton, T. & Keenan, T. (1991) Further analyses of the disposition argument in organizational behavior. *Journal of Applied Psychology*, **76**, 781–787.

Ones, D. S., Viswesvaran, C. & Schmidt, F. L. (1993) Comprehensive meta-analysis of integrity test validities: Findings and implications for personnel selection and theories of job performance. *Journal of Applied Psychology*, **78**, 679–703.

Robertson, I. T. (1993). Personality assessment and personnel selection. *European Review of Applied Psychology*, **43**, 187–194.

Robertson, I. T. & Downs, S. (1989) Work sample tests of trainability: A meta-analysis. *Journal of Applied Psychology*, **74**, 402–410.

Robertson, I. T. & Kinder, A. (1993). Personality and job competences: The criterion-related validity of some personality variables. *Journal of Occupational and Organizational Psychology*, **66**, 225–244.

Rotter, J. B. (1966) Generalized expectancies for internal vs external control of reinforcement. *Psychological Monographs*, **80** (Whole No. 609).

Saville and Holdsworth Ltd (1990) *Occupational Personality Questionnaire Manual*. Esher, Surrey: Saville and Holdsworth.

Schmitt, N., Gooding, R. Z., Noe, R. A. & Kirsch, M. (1984) Meta-analysis of validity studies published between 1964 and 1982 and the investigation of study characteristics. *Personnel Psychology*, **37**, 407–422.

Staw, B. M. & Ross, J. (1985) Stability in the midst of change: A dispositional approach to job attitudes. *Journal of Applied Psychology*, **70**, 469–525.

Tett, R. P., Jackson, D. N. & Rothstein, M. (1991) Personality measures as predictors of job performance: A meta-analytic review. *Personnel Psychology*, **44**, 703–742.

Warr, P. B. (1990) The measurement of well-being and other aspects of mental health. *Journal of Occupational Psychology*, **63**, 193–210.

Watson, D. & Clark, L. A. (1984) Negative affectivity: The disposition to experience aversive emotional states. *Psychological Bulletin*, **96**, 465–490.

Wiesner, W. H. & Cronshaw, S. F. (1988) A meta-analytic investigation of the impact of interview format and degree of structure on the validity of the employment interview. *Journal of Occupational Psychology*, **61**, 271–290.

CHAPTER 7

The Psychological Contract as an Explanatory Framework in the Employment Relationship

Lynn McFarlane Shore
Georgia State University, USA

and

Lois E. Tetrick
Wayne State University, USA

The relationship between employees and their organizations has often been described as an exchange relationship (Mowday, Porter & Steers, 1982), and many concepts have been set forth in the literature to describe this exchange (Eisenberger et al, 1986; Greenberg, 1990). The psychological contract (Argyris, 1960; Rousseau, 1989; Schein, 1980) is an exchange concept providing a broad explanatory framework for understanding employee–organization linkages. The purpose of this chapter is to explore the role of the psychological contract in organizations. It examines the meaning and function of the psychological contract, including factors that contribute to its formation. In addition, the different types of contracts which can emerge, and implications of violations of these various contracts, are discussed.

Trends in Organizational Behavior, Volume 1. Edited by C. L. Cooper and D. M. Rousseau
© 1994 John Wiley & Sons Ltd.

THE MEANING OF THE PSYCHOLOGICAL CONTRACT

Schein (1980) described the psychological contract as the depiction of the exchange relationship between the individual employee and the organization. The psychological contract is the employee's perception of the reciprocal obligations existing with their employer; as such, the employee has beliefs regarding the organization's obligations to them as well as their own obligations to the organization (Rousseau, 1989). For example, the employee may believe that the organization has agreed to certain actions, such as providing job security and promotional opportunities, in exchange for hard work and loyalty by the employee.

While the individual employee believes in the existence of a particular psychological contract, or reciprocal exchange agreement, this does not necessarily mean that the supervisor or other organizational members agree with or have the same understanding of the contract (Rousseau & Parks, 1993). The psychological contract is an inherently subjective phenomenon, in part due to individual cognitive and perceptual limits, but also because there are multiple sources of information which may influence the development and modification of contracts (Levinson, 1962).

The psychological contract is one type of promissory contract. The promissory contract consists of three components, including promise, payment, and acceptance (Rousseau & Parks, 1993). A promise consists of a commitment to a future course of action. As an individual-level phenomenon, the psychological contract is based on *perceived* promises by the organization to the employee. These promises can be communicated directly by organizational agents (e.g. recruiters, managers). A recruiter who emphasizes promotional opportunities may set the stage for a psychological contract even though the new hire knows the promotional decision would be made by someone else. However, perceptions of promises to the employee can also be based on organizational actions. For example, past or present treatment of the employee (e.g. training, praise) can create perceptions of obligations by the organization to continue such treatment (Eisenberger et al, 1986; Eisenberger, Fasolo & Davis-LaMastro, 1990).

Payment occurs when something is offered in exchange for the promise which the person values. When an organization rewards employees in a manner consistent with the perceived promises underlying the psychological contract, this constitutes fulfilment of organizational obligations. In sum, promises followed by employee effort lead to expectations of payment, or organizational fulfilment of obligations. This process creates psychological contracts which, when violated, may lead to strong negative feelings (Robinson & Rousseau, in press; Rousseau & Parks, 1993).

The third component of promissory contracts is acceptance, reflecting voluntary agreement to engage in the contract terms (Rousseau, 1989; Rousseau & Parks, 1993). Acceptance implies that both parties (employee and organization) are accountable for the terms of the psychological contract, since they chose to engage in this particular agreement. Therefore, both employees and organizations are responsible for carrying out the contract, and either party may choose to violate or break the agreement.

In sum, because of pervasive social norms of reciprocity (Gouldner, 1960) and contracting (Rousseau & Parks, 1993), acceptance of the contract terms by the employee and the implied or explicit acceptance by the employer, sets the stage for the development of a psychological contract. In a sense, the employee expects, looks for, and creates the psychological contract as a way of representing the employment relationship because of these pervasive social norms.

FUNCTION OF THE PSYCHOLOGICAL CONTRACT

Given the evidence supporting the existence of the psychological contract (Robinson, Kraatz & Rousseau, in 1994; Robinson & Rousseau, in press; Rousseau, 1990), an important issue has to do with what the function of the psychological contract is. It could be argued that these types of contracts occur because of the lack of formalized contracts (e.g. union contracts). However, in our view, even when a formalized contract is present, individuals will develop psychological contracts for a number of reasons. First, even though many employment contracts are quite comprehensive, it is not possible to work out all aspects of employment. Thus, psychological contracts reduce individual uncertainty by establishing agreed-upon conditions of employment. That is, employees have a greater sense of security by believing that they have an understood agreement with their employer. In addition, psychological contracts serve to direct employee behavior without necessarily requiring managerial surveillance. Since employees monitor their own behavior based on the belief that this will lead to certain rewards either in the short-term, or in the distant future, this helps to serve organizational needs for responsible employees. Finally, psychological contracts give employees the feeling that they are able to influence their destiny in the organization since they are party to the contract, having agreed to its terms, and also because they are able to choose whether to carry out their obligations.

A theme underlying the reasons outlined above for the formation of contracts is the reduction of uncertainty or conversely an increment in predictability. Formal or explicit contracts between two parties specify the obligations of each party to the contract. In the employment setting, it has been long recognized that formal contracts cannot eliminate all ambiguity (e.g. collective bargaining contract violations). One step removed from the formal contract is the implied contract. The implied contract results from observable patterns of behavior between parties (e.g. patterns of practice; Rousseau, 1989). Rousseau has added a third level of contracts operating at the individual, perceptual level (i.e. psychological contracts) consisting of reciprocal obligations between the employee and organization. Even though this is an individual phenomenon, it is our thesis that the psychological contract still serves a primary function of uncertainty reduction.

Many motivational theories propose that predictability and control of the work environment are key factors in understanding individuals' behavior within that work environment. For example, predictability is a key concept in expectancy theories of motivation in that an individual has to have a sense that there is at least some likelihood that performance will result in desired outcomes (Vroom, 1964). More recently, extensions of goal setting theory have incorporated the concept of self-efficacy indicating that the individual needs to have some sense of predictability, at least with respect to a given task, to accept goals and perform accordingly (Bandura & Cervone, 1983). Furthermore, Sutton and Kahn (1986) proposed that understanding, predictability, and control are key factors in preventing stress.

This raises the question as to how psychological contracts serve to increase control and predictability. Drawing on cognitive psychology, it has been proposed that people form schemas and scripts which are highly structured, pre-existing knowledge systems to interpret their organizational world and generate appropriate behaviors (Lord & Foti, 1986). These schemas and scripts can be thought of as individuals' belief structure of what is expected to occur in the organization and what is expected of them. If we liken schemas and scripts to the psychological contract then it would be expected that psychological contracts are relatively robust, once formed, and minor discrepancies would be overlooked (Fiske & Taylor, 1984). Further, while there has been only scant research on how schemas develop, Lord and Foti summarize that schemas develop out of repeated experiences and, as they develop, they become more abstract, complex, organized, and more resistant to change. Thus, psychological contracts represent schemas having to do with mutual obligations between the individual and their employer, which may be fairly simple at the time of organizational entry, but become increasingly complex with experience. As schemas, psychological contracts provide the employee with order and continuity in a complex employment relationship, allowing for predictability and control.

TRANSACTIONAL VERSUS RELATIONAL CONTRACTS

In their conceptual development of the psychological contract, Rousseau and her colleagues (Parks, 1992; Rousseau, 1989; Rousseau & Parks, 1993) distinguished between two forms of the psychological contract, called transactional and relational obligations. They linked the former type of contract with economic exchange and the latter type of contract with social exchange. Blau (1964; p.89) described social exchange theory in the following way: "An individual who supplies rewarding services to another obligates him. To discharge this obligation, the second must furnish benefits to the first in turn." Unlike economic exchange, social exchange "involves unspecified obligations, the fulfilment of which depends on trust because it cannot be enforced in the absence of a binding contract" (p.113). Emerson (1981) suggested that unlike social exchange theory, which focuses on contingent and reciprocal exchanges between partners, economic theory is based upon the assumption that transactions between parties are independent events (i.e. are not long-term and ongoing). As a result, "obligations, trust, interpersonal attachment, or commitment to specific exchange partners" (Emerson, 1981; p.35) are not incorporated into economic exchange frameworks (i.e. transactional psychological contracts).

DEVELOPMENT OF THE PSYCHOLOGICAL CONTRACT

Given that individuals may have substantially different psychological contracts, this raises questions as to how these varied contracts develop. Dunahee and Wangler (1974) suggested that psychological contracts initially emerge at the time of pre-employment negotiation. That is, not only are specific transactional agreements discussed (e.g. how much pay for amount of work), but also the nature and extent of obligations. However, they also argue that employees may infer contractual agreements without explicit communication by, for example, observing the employer's body language or based on their perceptions of the organization's characteristics. Thus, individuals seek information during recruitment and selection which then sets the stage for further refinement of the psychological contract in the early employment period. As such, the psychological contract develops within a dynamic environment in which the individual is often interacting with multiple organizational agents who may each be sending a variety of messages, both verbal and non-verbal. How then does the individual develop a psychological contract?

In our view, there are a number of factors operating. Potential employees and organizational agents approach the employment relationship with a set of expectations about the potential relationship. However, while these expectations do influence the development of the contract, the dynamic nature of the interaction between parties, the organization's goals and environmental conditions, and also the particular goal orientation of the individual who is developing the psychological contract, make the outcome of this exchange unique.

Figure 7.1 depicts a model showing how the psychological contract develops at the time of pre- and initial employment. There are two parties to the development of this contract—the individual and the organization. Consistent with interactional psychology (Endler & Magnusson, 1976; Terborg, 1981), we view the development of the psychological contract as resulting from the interaction of the individual

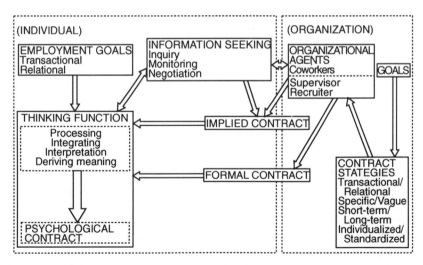

Figure 7.1 Schematic representation of the development of the psychological contract

with their organizational environment. Therefore, we propose that individuals are both shaped by situations and also shape situations; as such, the psychological contract is unique for individuals because of the interactional process. However, there are also forces that may encourage some similarity in psychological contracts among individuals within organizations (e.g. implied contracts and formal contracts). Below, we will first discuss the role of the individual, and then subsequently the role of organizational agents in the development of the psychological contract.

The Role of the Individual

There is much evidence that individuals behave in ways that are consistent with their goals (Cleveland & Murphy, 1992), and that information in the environment assumes meaning in part due to a person's goals (Ashford & Cummings, 1983). Ashford and Cummings argued that employees are active seekers of information about a wide variety of issues related to the goals they hope to achieve in a particular organization, such as job competence, career advancement, and making friends at work. The development of the psychological contract can be thought of as a deliberate goal-oriented process, in which an individual attempts to establish an agreement with their employing organization which will address a variety of employment objectives.

Figure 7.1 incorporates elements from the Ashford and Cummings (1983) feedback seeking model to explain the individual cognitive processes that underlie the development of the psychological contract. Individuals enter the employment relationship within a particular environment which contains a broad array of information. Our model proposes that people have goal-oriented motivations for seeking information relevant to the psychological contract. Both transactional and relational goals are likely to be motivators for information seeking. Transactional motivators consist of promotional opportunities, pay and benefits whereas relational motivators include job security, growth and development opportunities, and the interpersonal environment (Robinson et al, 1994).

The degree of emphasis on transactional and relational issues is likely to vary due to differences in individual goals. For example, a student who is seeking temporary employment with flexible working hours in order to accommodate her school schedule may be more interested in transactional aspects of her psychological contract, whereas another individual seeking long-term employment opportunities may focus on information relevant to the relational contract, including elements such as career development opportunities and job security. Thus, an individual's information-seeking efforts will be organized around their particular employment goals.

New hires, as well as more tenured employees, may use a variety of approaches to seeking information relevant to the psychological contract, including inquiry, monitoring, and negotiation. Direct inquiry and negotiation may be a chief means of gathering information about transactional issues such as pay and benefits. However, there may be many contractual issues that individuals may hesitate to ask about directly or which are not likely to be viewed as negotiable (e.g. the fairness of the supervisor, or the extent of support with personal problems). Nonetheless, if the individual is concerned about these relational issues, they will seek relevant information through the process of monitoring.

Individuals monitor their environment for information relevant to their goals; meaning is generated through the thinking function by incorporating environmental information into existing goals (Ashford & Cummings, 1983). Ashford and Cummings suggest that monitoring involves both "interpretation and inference... since the derived meaning of any feedback cue is in part a function of an individual's self- and goal-related schemas" (pp. 383–384). For example, if a manager discusses job security with a potential new hire who views the organization as a mere stepping stone in their career (Robinson & Rousseau, in press), this particular information will likely be ignored and will not be incorporated into the relational contract.

The development of the psychological contract involves not only the use of direct inquiry and monitoring, but also active attempts on the part of the individual to negotiate an agreement consistent with their employment goals. Negotiation is most likely to affect the formal employment contract (e.g. pay and benefits) in a direct way, but aspects of the formal contract are likely to influence the psychological contract. Similarly, inquiry and monitoring are likely to directly influence the implied contract, which in turn influences the psychological contract. Therefore, more explicit forms of contracting (formal and implied contracts) influence more implicit forms of contracting (psychological contracts). At the same time, all three information seeking strategies have a direct effect on the development of the psychological contract.

Given that individuals are likely to store and recall incomplete information, and also to fill in information based on existing schemas (Salancik & Pfeffer, 1978), new hires are likely to base their psychological contract on information which is only partially generated by the external environment. That is, individuals incorporate only some of the available information in the environment and then derive meaning from that information in their own unique way. Suppose that a new college graduate for whom career development is an important goal has never worked full time. He will probably interpret and utilize information on advancement opportunities in a manner quite different from a more experienced individual who has already worked for several organizations. Therefore, even if these two people were given the same information about advancement opportunities during an interview with a manager, they are likely to differ in how they make sense of the information presented. As a result, their psychological contracts pertaining to career development are also likely to be distinct.

The Role of the Organization

Organizations are made up of multiple individuals, with varying roles and perspectives. During recruitment and organizational entry, the individual interacts with a variety of people who may provide information for the development of the contract. In our view, there are forces which might encourage different organizational agents to send somewhat different messages. For example, there is a great deal of evidence that the majority of organizations attempt to "sell" the organization to recruits (Wanous, 1992), so that individuals may receive different messages at the time of recruitment than they would once they begin working for the organization. This may help to explain why so many new hires view their organizations as substantially violating their psychological contract early in the employment relationship (Robinson & Rousseau, in press). However, once a new hire enters the organization, there should be some continuity in the messages relayed given that organizations tend toward homogeneity in their work force through attraction–selection–attrition (Schneider, 1987) and socialization processes (Wanous, 1992). In addition, both formal and implied contracts lend some continuity to psychological contracts. Therefore, particular types of contracts might be prevalent within a given organization (Parks, 1992; Rousseau & Wade-Benzoni, in press; Tsui et al, 1993).

A number of researchers have proposed that organizational strategies are linked with employment contracts (Parks, 1992; Rousseau & Wade-Benzoni, in press; Tsui et al, 1993). For example, organizations in quickly changing environments may make a strategic decision to negotiate short-term temporary employment contracts with some of their employees (e.g. clerical workers). In contrast, customer-oriented organizations where building trust is essential to organizational profits, as in the banking industry, may offer long-term employment and development opportunities in employment contracts. Thus, organizations may have a predominant type of contract that typifies employee–organization relations.

Both Parks (1992) and Rousseau and Wade-Benzoni (in press) developed strategic typologies which represent refinements of the transactional and relational contracts described previously. Parks proposed that transactional and relational contracts may be either exhaustive (fully described) or fragmentary (incomplete and uncertain). Rousseau and Wade-Benzoni's typology uses the dimensions of duration (short-term versus long-term) and performance terms (specified and not specified) to create four types of contracts. Tsui et al (1993) proposed that organizations may develop job-focused strategies or organization-focused strategies. The job-focused strategy involves a very specific contract in which both employee and organizational obligations are made very explicit. It is a flexible contract in which neither the employee nor organization is committed beyond the specified contract period. The organization-focused strategy is much less specific, and involves employee commitments to invest in both the job and organization in exchange for long-term returns from the organization. This typology is very similar to the transactional and relational contract distinction utilized by Rousseau (1989).

There are several themes in the strategic contract typologies described above which are incorporated into Figure 7.1. First, contracts differ on the extent to which they are *specific*. *Duration* of the contract, reflecting the degree to which it involves investments and long-term relationships, is a second dimension of contracts. Third, contracts vary as to whether they are *transactional or relational*. Like Rousseau and Wade-Benzoni (in press), we view this dimension as existing on a continuum, such that most contracts involve both monetizeable and nonmonetizeable elements, though the weight given to these elements may be quite varied. A final issue that has not been discussed is the degree to which contracts are *individualized versus standardized*. Some organizations may employ fairly uniform strategies in negotiating contracts with employees. This represents an egalitarian strategy which should contribute to group cohesiveness (Kabanoff, 1991). Other organizations may individualize contracts to represent potential contributions to the organization. That is, better employees may negotiate contracts that will provide them with more rewards and greater opportunities. This represents an equity strategy, in which rewards and opportunities are distributed according to employee contributions (Kabanoff, 1991).

The goals of the organization should also impact the development of the psychological contract. Organizations facing a great deal of competition for their services or products may seek to establish more transactionally oriented contracts of short duration, consistent with a goal to be flexible and responsive to a changing environment. In contrast, organizations that have a goal of building strong customer relations may opt for more open-ended relational contracts of longer duration. As yet, little is known about the impact of organizational goals on the contract development process. However, recent organizational trends toward contract workers, temporary employment as well as early retirement incentive programs in reaction to economic pressures suggest that organizational goals will be related to the type of contract that emerges.

Various organizational sources may play different roles in the contract development process. Presumably, prior to organizational entry, an individual will develop their psychological contract based on the organizational agents they interact with, usually a recruiter or other human resource department representative, and their immediate supervisor or manager. However, prior to talking with organizational agents, the individual may already have information about a particular organization through a variety of sources (e.g. news media, friends and family) relevant to the psychological contract. For example, knowledge of a recent early retirement incentive program offered by a particular company may contribute to aspects of the contract having to do with long-term job security.

Research suggests that the recruiter is not considered a very credible source of information (Fisher, Ilgen & Hoyer, 1979) while newcomers often rely extensively on their supervisor (Fisher, 1990). In addition, the individual will have to depend on their immediate supervisor to carry out many of the contract terms. Therefore, the employee is likely to view the supervisor as the chief agent for establishing and maintaining the psychological contract.

There is much evidence that coworkers play an important informational role in the socialization process (Fisher, 1990; Miller & Jablin, 1991). Coworkers may be useful sources of information about the psychological contract in a number of ways. First, coworkers may share their perceptions of the "fairness" of the supervisor and the "trustworthiness" of the organization (relational issues that are hard to assess during recruitment), so that the new hire is able to revise their contract or at least estimate the likelihood of violation. Second, coworkers may be a source of information about how equitable the new hire's contract is relative to others. This can occur through direct communications about salary or other aspects of the contract (e.g. was the employee paid fairly relative to others, do excellent performers really get promoted), or through observation of interactions among coworkers or between coworkers and the supervisor.

VIOLATION OF THE PSYCHOLOGICAL CONTRACT

The psychological contract once developed should be relatively stable. However, this does not imply that it cannot be changed. Rather, the psychological contract is based on an interactive process by which the employee takes steps to fulfil their part of the contract and looks to the organization to fulfil their obligations within the terms of the contract. We view the psychological contract as the standard or referent against which an individual judges the employment relationship as suggested by self-regulation theories of motivation and control theory (Carver & Scheier, 1985; Kanfer, 1990). To the extent that the present employment situation is not consistent with the standard (i.e. the employee views the contract as violated), control theory suggests that an individual will respond to reduce the discrepancy (Kernan & Lord, 1990).

Robinson and Rousseau (in press) reported that violations of the contract are the norm rather than the exception with 59% of the respondents in a study reporting that their employer had violated the contract. The relation between individuals reporting that the contract had been violated and the extent to which the obligations of the employer to the employee had been fulfilled was negative. Interestingly, there were individuals who reported that the contract had been violated who also indicated that their employer had lived up to their obligations. Likewise, there were individuals who indicated that the contract had not been violated even though they reported that the employer's obligations had not been fulfilled. Robinson and Rousseau suggest that this seeming discrepancy might be explained, at least in part, by efforts to resolve disputes. Drawing on self-regulation theories of motivation, we offer additional explanations of the process that occurs when an individual senses that the obligations of the employer are not being met.

Figure 7.2 depicts the process underlying violation of the psychological contract. Violation of the psychological contract is a reactive process whereby the employee receives information from the organization which suggests that an obligation within the contract terms has not been met. Although we describe violation as a reactive process, in reality, the employee may have contributed to organizational actions which led to contract violation. However, as suggested by Murphy and Cleveland (1991), people tend to discount their own poor performance by making allowances for situational influences. Thus, even a poorly performing or disruptive employee may not view themselves as having a responsibility in organizational violations of contracts. As such, we are describing the individual's perceptions of contract violation, rather than incorporating all of the variables that may precipitate contract violation.

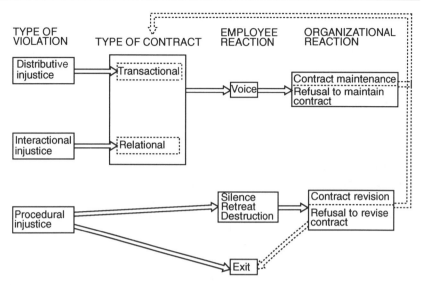

Figure 7.2 Schematic representation of the response to violation of the psychological contract

Since employees monitor the information environment at work to gain goal-related feedback (Ashford & Cummings, 1983), many of the discrepancies between the psychological contract and organizational actions will likely be attended to. However, the degree to which employees focus on discrepancies will depend on (1) the type of violation, (2) the size of the discrepancy, and (3) the degree of assessed organizational responsibility for the unmet obligations. Below, we will discuss each of these three aspects of unmet obligations.

Drawing from the organizational justice literature (c.f. Bies, 1987; Greenberg, 1990; Sweeney & McFarlin, 1993), we propose that there are several potential types of organizational violations. That is, like justice, violation involves an assessment of fairness by the employee. This assessment may focus on distributive violations which refer to the distribution of outcomes (e.g. training and merit pay). Unfulfilled transactional obligations would most often be associated with distributive violations since transactional contracts focus on specific monetizeable outcomes. However, the relational contract may also incorporate certain desired outcomes, such as job security, which if violated, would be evaluated in terms of distributive justice.

Procedural justice refers to the fairness of procedures through which outcomes are allocated. If a tenured employee were part of a layoff, their assessments of violation would not only focus on the outcome (being laid off), but also on how the layoff decision was made. The employee would likely perceive that a procedural violation had occurred if a coworker with lower tenure had been retained. A final aspect of justice is interactional justice, which Bies (1987) described as "quality of interpersonal treatment they receive during the implementation of a procedure" (p. 292). The tenured employee described above might also feel that an interactional violation had occurred if he was notified of the layoff through an impersonal form letter. Interactional violations are particularly relevant to relational contracts, where trust is an essential part of the agreement.

Another issue related to the type of violation which may influence employee reactions is whether the psychological contract is chiefly transactional or relational. Reactions to violation of contracts that are primarily transactional, particularly of short duration, may be less intense and more amenable to revision than violation of long-standing relational contracts where employees are relying on mutual trust (Robinson et al, 1994).

The second aspect of violations that will influence employee reactions is the size of the discrepancy. Certain violations may result in larger discrepancies than others. According to action control theory (Kuhl & Atkinson, 1986), small discrepancies would be expected to generate an action orientation which in the case of the psychological contract would lead to employee attempts to restore the contract. Large discrepancies, on the other hand, would be expected to induce a state orientation which would result in the individual focusing on the emotional effects of the violation of the contract. This is consistent with Rousseau's (1989) thesis that violations of psychological contracts lead to not only perceptions of inequity and dissatisfaction but also "deeper and more intense responses, akin to anger and moral outrage" (p. 128).

The third aspect of violations that may influence employee reactions is accountability, or assessed responsibility for unmet obligations. According to Bies (1987), people make attributions of responsibility when they make judgements of fairness. If an organization appears to break the psychological contract voluntarily, judgements of injustice may be greater than when the organization is not held to be fully responsible. For example, a psychological contract representing organizational obligations of job security in exchange for employee obligations to be loyal, which is broken (e.g. when an employee is fired or part of a layoff) may be viewed as only a partially broken contract if an economic downturn caused the organization to be unable to fulfil the obligation. In addition, when the organization claims that they cannot completely fulfil a contract, but attempts to partially do so (e.g. early voluntary retirement rather than a layoff), this voluntary attempt may lessen perceptions of a violated contract.

An integration of action control theory and the organizational justice literature suggests that for individuals with transactional contracts, the most salient violations will be those resulting from distributive injustice (Greenberg, 1990), and interactional injustices (Bies, 1987) may be discounted unless the discrepancy is very large. Procedural injustice in conjunction with distributive injustice would exacerbate the effect of distributive injustice and increase the likelihood of the individual adopting a state orientation. Similarly, for individuals with relational contracts, the most salient violations will be procedural and interactional injustices, and distributive injustices may be discounted unless the discrepancy is very large. Procedural injustice in conjunction with interactional injustice would be expected to compound the impact of the violation and result in a state orientation being adopted. Therefore, one would expect different responses to the violation of psychological contracts based on the type and size of the discrepancy depending on whether the psychological contract is primarily a transactional or relational contract.

Based on work by Robinson (1993), Figure 7.2 incorporates five potential employee responses to violation: (1) voice, (2) silence, (3) retreat, (4) destruction, and (5) exit. Voice is consistent with an action orientation involving attempts to maintain or reinstate the psychological contract. In contrast, silence, retreat, destruction and exit are more consistent with a state orientation, in which the employee attempts to survive contract violation by lowering perceived obligations of the employer, of themselves to the employer, or withdrawing from the employment relationship. Therefore, perceived distributive injustices under conditions of a transactional contract would result in voice responses which if unsuccessful would lead to silence, retreat, destruction, and eventually exit from the organization. Similarly, the perception of interactional injustices under conditions of a relational contract would result in voice responses which if unsuccessful would result in silence, retreat, or destruction; this is reflective of moving to a more transactional contract and potentially exit from the organization. However, if these perceptions were accompanied with procedural injustice or the discrepancies are large, then individuals may not exercise voice regardless of the type of contract but would be more likely to exercise silence, retreat, destruction, or exit. The limited research on violations of psychological contracts is consistent with this interpretation in that violations have been found to be negatively related to trust, organizational citizenship behaviors, employees' relational obligations, and employee withdrawal behaviors (Robinson et al, 1994; Robinson & Morrison, 1993; Robinson & Rousseau, in press).

CONCLUSIONS

Although contracts have received limited attention in the organizational behavior and human resource management research literatures, they are a very important element of the employment relationship. And yet, organizations may make strategic business decisions which result in serious contract violations often without an awareness of the implications for organizational viability. Although organizational justice provides some understanding of the dynamics of these strategic decisions in relation to employees, an element which has often been neglected is the type of psychological contract under which individuals are operating.

In Sutton's (1990) work on organizational decline processes, he discussed work force reduction in terms of both short- and long-term effects. He suggested that employees at all levels will experience anxiety and stress; lower level employees because they fear loss of jobs, higher level employees (managers) because they make the decisions about layoffs, transfers, and demotions. Psychological contracts, which provide employees with a sense of predictability and control, represent a means of explaining employee reactions to these types of organizational events. That is, both employees and managers recognize the loss of control and trust inherent in breaking long standing contracts. Further, the damage that work force reductions have on implied contracts (e.g. job security for tenure and loyalty) has been established in a number of studies (Brockner, 1988; Brockner et al, 1987; Rousseau & Anton, 1988, 1991; Rousseau & Aquino, 1993). Employees base their psychological contract in part on implied contracts, so that work force reductions, even when an employee is not directly affected, can do serious damage to the psychological contract.

Work force reductions and use of contract workers (Pearce, 1993) provide information to employees about the type of contract they have with the organization, as well as the likelihood of violation by the organization. Employees who feel that the organization has not carried out their obligations in important areas are likely to revise their contract substantially such that they may become poorer organizational citizens (Robinson & Morrison, 1993), and move to a more transactional contract with its focus on short-term specific obligations (Rousseau, 1989; Tsui et al, 1993). As such, substantial breaking of contracts may contribute to organizational decline at a time when the organization most needs the efforts of remaining employees. In a time of downsizing, layoffs, and early retirement incentives, understanding the meaning of the psychological contract and the role it plays in organizational success and failure is of paramount importance.

This raises the question as to why such limited research has been conducted on psychological contracts, given its potential impact on employees and organizations. One reason probably has to do with the individuality of the psychological contract. The issues that are incorporated into the contract, and the emphasis of these issues, are quite varied for individuals. A second reason may be that the psychological contract is not a static phenomenon, so that its meaning and impact may change and evolve over time, people, and situations. This makes it difficult to study and understand psychological contracts. Nonetheless, recent conceptual (Rousseau, 1989; Rousseau & Parks, 1993; Rousseau & Wade-Benzoni, in press) and empirical work (Robinson et al, 1994; Robinson & Rousseau, in press; Robinson & Morrison, 1993) provides direction for future research on the psychological contract. Based on this early research, it is clear that the psychological contract is an important organizational phenomenon which provides a basis for understanding the link between employees and their organizations.

REFERENCES

Argyris, C. P. (1960) *Understanding Organizational Behavior*. Homewood, IL: Dorsey Press.

Ashford, S. J. & Cummings, L. L. (1983) Feedback as an individual resource: Personal strategies of creating information. *Organizational Behavior and Human Performance*, **32**, 370–398.

Bandura, A. & Cervone, D. (1983) Self-evaluative and self-efficacy mechanisms governing the motivational effects of goal systems. *Journal of Personality and Social Psychology*, **45**, 1017–1028.

Bies, R. J. (1987) The predicament of injustice: The management of moral outrage. *Research in Organizational Behavior*, **9**, 289–319.

Blau, P. M. (1964) *Exchange and Power in Social Life*. New York: John Wiley.

Brockner, J. (1988) The effects of work layoffs on survivors: Research, theory, and practice. *Research in Organizational Behavior*, **10**, 213–255.

Brockner, J., Grover, S., Reed, T., DeWitt, R. & O'Malley, M. (1987) Survivors reactions to layoffs: We get by with a little help for our friends. *Administrative Science Quarterly*, **32**, 526–541.

Carver, C. S. & Scheier, M. F. (1985) A control-systems approach to the self-regulation of action. In J. Kuhl & J. Beckmann (Eds.) *Action Control: From Cognition to Behavior*. New York: Springer-Verlag, pp.237–266.

Cleveland, J. N. & Murphy, K. R. (1992) Analyzing performance appraisal as goal-directed behavior. *Research in Personnel and Human Resource Management*, **10**, 121–185.

Dunahee, M. H. & Wangler, L. A. (1974) The psychological contract: A conceptual structure for management/employee relations. *Personnel Journal*, July, 518–526, 548.

Eisenberger, R., Fasolo, P. & Davis-LaMastro, V. (1990) Perceived organizational support and employee diligence, commitment, and innovation. *Journal of Applied Psychology*, **75**, 51–59.

Eisenberger, R., Huntington, R., Hutchison, S. & Sowa, D. (1986) Perceived organizational support. *Journal of Applied Psychology*, **71**, 500–507.

Emerson, R. (1981) Social exchange theory. In M. Rosenberg & R. Turner (Eds.), *Social Psychology: Sociological Perspectives*. New York: Basic Books, pp. 30–65.

Endler, N. S. & Magnusson, D. (1976) Toward an interactional psychology of personality. *Psychological Bulletin*, **83**, 956–974.

Fisher, C. D. (1990) Organizational socialization: An integrative view. In G. R. Ferris & K. M. Rowland (Eds.) *Career and Human Resources Development*. Greenwich, CT: JAI Press.

Fisher, C. D., Ilgen, D. R. & Hoyer, W. D. (1979) Source credibility, information favorability and job offer acceptance. *Academy of Management Journal*, **22**, 94–103.

Fiske, S. T. & Taylor, S. E. (1984) *Social Cognition*. Reading, MA: Addison-Wesley.

Gouldner, A. W. (1960) The norm of reciprocity. *American Sociological Review*, **25**, 165–167.

Greenberg, J. (1990) Organizational justice: Yesterday, today, and tomorrow. *Journal of Management*, **16**, 399–432.

Kabanoff, B. (1991) Equity, equality, power, and conflict. *Academy of Management Review*, **16**, 416–441.

Kanfer, R. (1990) Motivation theory and industrial and organizational psychology. In M. D. Dunnette & L. Hough (Eds.) *Handbook of Industrial & Organizational Psychology*, Second Edition, Vol. 1, pp. 75–170. Palo Alto, CA: Consulting Psychologists Press.

Kernan, M. C. & Lord, R. G. (1990) The effect of valence, expectancies, and goal-performance discrepancies in single and multiple goal environments. *Journal of Applied Psychology*, **75**, 194–203.

Kuhl, J. & Atkinson, J. W. (1986) *Motivation, Thought, and Action*. New York: Praeger.

Levinson, H. (1962) *Men, Management and Mental Health*. Cambridge, MA: Harvard University Press.

Lord, R. G. & Foti, R. J. (1986) Schema theories, information processing, and organizational behaviors. In H. P. Sims, Jr, D. A. Gioia & Associates (Eds.) *The Thinking Organization*. San Francisco: Jossey-Bass.

Miller, V. D. & Jablin, F. M. (1991) Information seeking during organizational entry: Influences, tactics, and a model of the process. *Academy of Management Review*, **16**, 92–120.

Mowday, R. T., Porter, L. W. & Steers, R. M. (1982) *Employee–Organization Linkages: The Psychology of Commitment, Absenteeism and Turnover*. New York: Academic Press.

Murphy, K. R. & Cleveland, J. N. (1991) *Performance Appraisal: An Organizational Perspective*. Boston: Allyn & Bacon.

Parks, J. M. (1992) The role of incomplete contracts and their governance in delinquency, in-role, and extra-role behaviors. Paper presented at the Society for Industrial and Organizational Psychology, Montreal.

Pearce, J. L. (1993) Toward an organizational behavior of contract laborers: Their psychological involvement and effects on employee coworkers. *Academy of Management Journal*, **36**, 1082–1096.

Robinson, S. L. (1993) Monkey see, monkey do: Dissatisfaction behavior from a social information processing perspective. Paper presented at the Eighth Annual conference of the Society for Industrial and Organizational Psychology, San Francisco.

Robinson, S. & Morrison, E. W. (1993) The effect of contract violation on organizational citizenship behavior. Unpublished manuscript, New York University.

Robinson, S. L. & Rousseau, D. M. (in press) Violating the psychological contract: Not the exception but the norm. *Journal of Organizational Behavior*.

Robinson, S. L., Kraatz, M. S. & Rousseau, D. M. (1994) Changing obligations and the psychological contract: A longitudinal study. *Academy of Management Journal*, **37**, 137–152.

Rousseau, D. M. (1989) Psychological and implied contracts in organizations. *Employee Responsibilities and Rights Journal*, **2**, 121–139.

Rousseau, D. M. (1990) New hire perceptions of their own and their employer's obligations: A study of psychological contracts. *Journal of Organizational Behavior*, **11**, 389–400.

Rousseau, D. M. & Anton, R. J. (1988) Fairness and implied contract obligations in job terminations: A policy-capturing study. *Human Performance*, **1**, 273–289.

Rousseau, D. M. & Anton, R. J. (1991) Fairness and implied contract obligations in job terminations: The role of contributions, promises, and performance. *Journal of Organizational Behavior*, **12**, 287–299.

Rousseau, D. M. & Aquino, K. (1993) Fairness and implied contract obligations in job terminations: The role of remedies, social accounts, and procedural justice. *Human Performance*, **6**, 135–149.

Rousseau, D. M. & Parks, J. M. (1993) The contracts of individuals and organizations. *Research in Organizational Behavior*, **15**, 1–43.

Rousseau, D. M. & Wade-Benzoni, K. (in press) Linking strategy and human resource practices: How employee and customer contracts are created. *Human Resource Management*.

Salancik, G. R. & Pfeffer, J. (1978) A social information processing approach to job attitudes and task design. *Administrative Science Quarterly*, **23**, 224–253.

Schein, E. H. (1980) *Organizational Psychology*. Englewood Cliffs, NJ: Prentice-Hall.

Schneider, B. (1987) The people make the place. *Personnel Psychology*, **40**, 437–453.

Sutton, R. I. (1990) Organizational decline processes: A social psychological perspective. *Research in Organizational Behavior*, **12**, 205–253.

Sutton, R. & Kahn, R. L. (1986) Prediction, understanding, and control as antidotes to organizational stress. In J. Lorsch (Ed.) *Handbook of Organizational Behavior*. Englewood Cliffs, NJ: Prentice-Hall.

Sweeney, P. D. & McFarlin, D. B. (1993) Worker's evaluations of the "ends" and the "means": An examination of four models of distributive and procedural justice. *Organizational Behavior and Human Decision Processes*, **55**, 23–40.

Terborg, J. R. (1981) Interactional psychology and research on human behavior in organizations. *Academy of Management Review*, **6**, 569–576.

Tsui, A. S., Porter, L. W., Pearce, J. L. & Tripoli, A. M. (1993) Reconceptualizing the employee–organization relationship: An inducement-contribution approach. Unpublished manuscript, University of California, Irvine.

Vroom, V. H. (1964) *Work and Motivation*. New York: John Wiley.

Wanous, J. P. (1992) *Recruitment, Selection, Orientation and Socialization of Newcomers*. Second edition. New York: Addison-Wesley.

CHAPTER 8

"Till Death Us Do Part . . ." Changing Work Relationships in the 1990s

Judi McLean Parks
Industrial Relations Center, University of Minnesota and Cornell University, USA

and

Deborah L. Kidder
Industrial Relations Center, University of Minnesota, USA

. . . from this day forward, for better for worse, for richer for poorer, in sickness and in health . . . till death us do part . . (Church of England, 1750)

INTRODUCTION

Commitments are the stuff of dreams, and the glue that bind one person to another in a relationship. Yet in organizations, the nature of our commitments to one another—employee to employee, employee to employer, and employer to employee—is changing. And the nature of these commitments may never again be the same. Over the last several years, economic conditions, in combination with what may be a short-run myopic focus on the part of many organizations, may have rung the death knell of the "organization man" (White, 1956), who once recited the mantra:

Trends in Organizational Behavior, Volume 1. Edited by C. L. Cooper and D. M. Rousseau
© 1994 John Wiley & Sons Ltd.

> Be loyal to the company and the company will be loyal to you. After all, if
> you do a good job for the organization, it is only good sense for the
> organization to be good to you, because that will be best for everybody.
> (White, 1956; p. 129)

In today's business environment, this mantra may be more wishful
thinking than truism. The nature of employment relationships is
changing. It may no longer be the case that employees can count on lifetime employment if they do their jobs well. Companies, faced with fierce
competition, bloated bureaucracies and high fixed labor costs, have cut
layers of management and laid off thousands of workers. A decade of
down-sizing and layoffs, more palatably termed "rightsizing", has left
the majority of workers—survivors or victims—feeling insecure
(Brockner et al, 1992) and has left many with broken psychological
contracts (e.g. McLean Parks & Schmedemann, 1992; Robinson, Kraatz &
Rousseau, 1994; Wiesenfeld & Brockner, 1993).

Many laid-off workers are being replaced with temporary workers.
The Bureau of Labor Statistics gauges the number of persons in the
temporary agency industry at about 1.4 million (Nardone, 1993), making
up at least 25% of the current workforce (Ansberry, 1993; Swardson,
1992). Some projections indicate that the workforce will be more than
50% contingent by the year 2000 (Dillin, 1993). Although attempts are
made to cast a positive light on these work arrangements through the
rhetoric of autonomy (Negrey, 1990; Smith, 1983), in reality, many of
these changes are being promoted by employers, leaving employees who
want jobs facing a 'take it or leave it' situation. Organizations justify the
use of temporary workers as a mechanism to increase flexibility in a
competitive environment. However, they may have done so at the cost of
productivity and quality, as well as specific human capital, lower levels
of internalized organizational values, and teamwork. As the nature of
the employment contract has changed, so have the behaviors that
employers can expect from employees.

Frequently the amount of work to be done does not decrease when
employees are laid off, but rather surviving employees are expected to
pick up the slack, working harder for their paychecks (Schor, 1992).
"Core" or permanent employees may bear some costs of the contingent
workforce as well in the form of increased responsibility and
performance expectations (Diesenhouse, 1993). Competitive pressures
are clearly leading organizations to place greater demands on employees
for "increased commitment, initiative, and flexibility" (Schor, 1992, p.19).
Seventy-five percent of the CEOs in a recent *Fortune* survey indicated
that economic conditions and the increasingly global economy will
require them to push their employees harder. They report that they will
make increased productivity and time demands on their employees,

although this is likely to result in an "overworked American" (Schor, 1992).[1] Schor (1992, p.19) quotes one executive as stating "[p]eople who work for me should have phones in their bathrooms", suggesting that organizations are intruding more and more into the private lives and time of their employees, but offering little in exchange.

In addition to the shift towards a more contingent and overworked workforce, we have also seen another trend in the last decade: specifically, an increase in violence and other detrimental behaviors in the workplace. It has been estimated that American business loses over $40 billion annually from employee theft (Hartnett, 1991; US Congress, 1990). In addition, mass murders in the workplace increased 200–300% over the last decade (Stuart, 1992). According to the National Institute for Occupational Safety and Health (NIOSH), homicide was the third leading cause of occupational death in the US from 1980 to 1988, and it is the leading cause of workplace death among female workers in the United States (Kedjidjian, 1993). Given workplace changes noted above, perhaps the profile of the typical workplace murderer should come as no surprise: middle aged, Caucasian male, who has recently been laid off (Stuart, 1992). The more involved employees are in their jobs and the more their identities are tied up in their jobs, the more they will feel the effects of a layoff. For these employees, a layoff is more than a loss of income. It is often equated with the *actual loss of their reason for being*. "When viewed in this light, violence committed by such individuals is no longer an irrational, random event. It becomes the logical consequence of the employee's job loss" (Stuart, 1992; p.74).

Each trend suggests serious issues towards which organizational scholars should turn their attention. What are the implications of the new work relationships for both *employee* and *employer?* What are the long range consequences of this new era of employment relationships? What behaviors can we expect from these employees as their contribution in exchange for the reduced inducements offered by the organization? In this chapter, we will explore these questions through the lenses of several established areas of research. The paper is divided into three parts. In the first, we will discuss the deployment of resources, or contributions, that employees may give to their employers. We will expand the organizational citizenship behavior (OCB) construct to include not only the behaviors which, in the aggregate are *beneficial* to the organization (Organ, 1988), but also those behaviors (e.g. theft and sabotage) which are *detrimental* to the organization. Resources may be either offered or withdrawn, and we will suggest that the contributory behaviors exemplified by OCBs have a mirror image which becomes apparent as the employee withdraws or withholds contributions to the organization when her or his psychological contract has been violated. Next, we will discuss psychological contracts. Specifically, we will examine the psychological contract of the employee as one way to understand the effects of these trends on employee behavior. Psychological contracts are inherently in the eye of the beholder (Rousseau & McLean Parks, 1993). These psychological contracts range from the transactional, emphasizing short time frames and economic benefit, to the relational, with diffuse obligations and extended time frames. Our perspective is that of the *employee*. Although *employer* reactions are also of interest, they are outside the focus of our paper. Finally, we will examine the implications in terms of the losses incurred through contract violation.

DOING MORE—OR LESS—THAN REQUIRED

What are the potential contributions which employees make in return for the inducements offered by the employer? Employees can choose to contribute those behaviors delineated by their job roles. Or they can invest additional energy and personal resources by going beyond role requirements. In this section, our discussion will be guided by the research which examines behaviors which go beyond delineated job requirements, and, more specifically, that of organizational citizenship behavior. Then, drawing from several perspectives, we will also examine what we believe to be the negative, mirror image of these extra-role, pro-organizational behaviors: anti-role behaviors.

Organizational Role Behaviors

Employees generally offer particular behaviors to the firm. The actual breadth of behaviors employees contribute depends on the types of inducements the organization offers (e.g. Simon, 1976), and how the job role itself has been defined and perceived (e.g. Van Dyne, Cummings & McLean Parks, 1995; Kidder & McLean Parks, 1993). However, these behaviors have a common characteristic: they either maintain the existing role (e.g. comply with requirements of the role or psychological contract) or enhance it (e.g. go beyond requirements). Behaviors which go beyond delineated requirements are "pro"-role, in the sense that they either maintain or enhance the performance of the behavioral expectations of the role.

Pro-role Behaviors: Role Maintenance and Enhancement

It has long been noted that organizations have a need for behaviors which go beyond role requirements (e.g. Barnard, 1938; Katz & Kahn,

1978). Recognizing the difficulty (if not impossibility) of anticipating all possible contingencies and delineating the requisite responses, researchers have become interested in defining these behaviors, and identifying their antecedents and consequences. Although there are a variety of constructs and conceptualizations of such behaviors, our focus is on organizational citizenship behavior as arguably the best known and most heavily researched (Van Dyne et al, 1995). Organ (1988) suggests that when performed in the aggregate, these behaviors are beneficial to the firm. Each characteristic citizenship behavior can be argued as either maintaining (e.g. compliance) or expanding/enhancing (e.g. altruism) the organizational role, and in that sense, are pro-role behaviors.

We introduce the terminology of pro-role behavior at the risk of creating even one more term in the domain of citizenship behavior research, an area which has been criticized for the plethora of terminology which is used (e.g. Van Dyne et al, 1995). However, our reasons for doing so will, we hope, shortly become apparent. In the context of the present paper, we believe that the term pro-role behavior has advantages over the predominant characterizations in the literature (i.e. extra-role behavior, prosocial organizational behavior, and organizational spontaneity). Specifically, the term "extra"-role (e.g. Katz & Kahn, 1978; Van Dyne et al, 1995) is frequently used to describe behaviors which go beyond role requirements. Yet several scholars note it is difficult to draw the line between in- and extra-role organizational behavior (e.g. George, 1991; Kidder & McLean Parks, 1993; Van Dyne et al, 1995). The ambiguity between in- and extra-role behavior may be interesting in and of itself. However, it is tangential to the issues addressed here. A related term, "prosocial" organizational behavior (e.g. Brief & Motowildo, 1986), conceptualizes these behaviors as actions of a prosocial nature which occur in organizations. This conceptualization does not specify that the behavior is oriented towards the organization and the execution of organizational roles, merely that it occurs in an organizational context. Finally, the term "organizational spontaneity" (e.g. George & Brief, 1992), for our purposes, is somewhat misleading. "Spontaneity" implies an impulsive character, belying the calculative and instrumental nature of many such behaviors. Thus, we will use the term *pro-role*, to emphasize the role expanding/enhancing flavor of citizenship behaviors. This will emphasize the contrast between these behaviors and *"anti"-role* behaviors (e.g. shirking, theft) which we explicate later in this paper, behaviors which either detract from or suspend the execution of role behaviors.

The organizational citizenship literature has focused on six constructs: *compliance, conscientiousness, sportsmanship, courtesy, civic virtue,* and *altruism. Compliance* is conformance with the requirements of one's job, and is typically operationalized as attendance and on-time performance. It is the execution of requisite behaviors, and is important in terms of whether or not coordination can be successfully achieved. *Conscientiousness* is more proactive in orientation. According to Organ (1988), conscientiousness is conforming to contracted (in-role) behaviours, but *beyond* minimum required standards. Behaviors such as superior attendance and overt diligence have been described as conscientious (e.g. Organ, 1988). *Sportsmanship* emphasizes restraint and forbearance, and includes behaviors such as focusing on what is right with the firm and avoiding complaining. *Courtesy* includes keeping co-workers informed or taking active steps to avoid potential problems (Organ, 1988); while *civic virtue* includes behaviors such as participation in meetings and training, and making active efforts to keep informed on matters that may be of benefit to the organization. Finally, *altruism* is characterized by helping another employee with their task (Organ, 1988); for example, helping a colleague catch up after an illness (Organ, 1988).

The degree to which each construct represents a facet of required performance is open to some debate (e.g. George, 1991; Kidder & McLean Parks, 1993; Van Dyne et al, 1995), and where required behaviors shade into the domain of voluntary behaviors is ambiguous. The line between them seems particularly blurred when discussing conscientiousness.[2] For our purposes, each of these six dimensions falls under the general rubric of a contribution which the employee can make to the organization in exchange for organizational inducements. These six constructs are simultaneously similar and dissimilar. Their commonality lies in the fact that it is assumed that these behaviors, when performed in the aggregate, will improve organizational performance (Organ, 1988) and in that they represent potential contributions by the employee to organizational effectiveness. With the exception of compliance, which is overtly in-role, each behavior also shares three other characteristics discussed by Hart (1988) as benevolent: they are (1) disinterested (i.e. personal gain is not the predominant motivation), (2) voluntary, and (3) intentional. Their difference lies in the nature of the behavior and the intensity of the underlying motivation.

Compliance is necessary as the delineated requirements of one's job. Dependable, in-role performance is important in terms of coordination and basic organizational functioning. Beyond compliance, however, we have conscientiousness, which is characterized as additional effort towards role requirements. Sportsmanship represents a form of behavior characterized by forbearance or restraint, or a withholding of potentially negative behaviors. In contrast to sportsmanship, each of the remaining behaviors implies a proactive, positive orientation, albeit perhaps with varying levels of intensity. Whether or not these behaviors can be arranged along a continuum from the task oriented focus of compliance and conscientiousness to the proactive supportiveness of altruism is an empirical question. However, intuitively, they would seem to lie on such a continuum ranging from the passive to the active, from least to most intensely oriented towards helping the organization—from a minimum to a maximum level of effort and contribution. Thus we might predict that the more committed and more involved an employee is in his or her job, the more intensely s/he is likely to contribute to the organization through these pro-role behaviors. This continuum is represented in Figure 8.1a, ranging from a minimal contribution to a maximal contribution, from compliance to altruism.

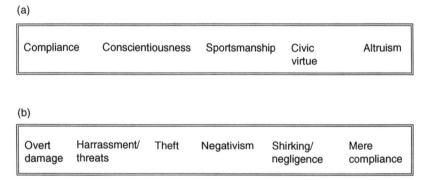

(a)

| Compliance | Conscientiousness | Sportsmanship | Civic virtue | Altruism |

(b)

| Overt damage | Harrassment/ threats | Theft | Negativism | Shirking/ negligence | Mere compliance |

Figure 8.1 Work behavior continua. **a**, Continuum of role and pro-role behaviors (OCBs). **b**, Continuum of anti-role behaviors

A steady stream of research over the last decade would support the contention that contracts with longer time frames (e.g. tenure), higher quality social and exchange relationships (e.g. leader behaviors and group cohesiveness; relationship orientation) and higher commitment levels, are more likely to produce pro-role behaviors (see Van Dyne et al, 1995, for a review).

"Anti"-role Behaviors: Role Detraction and Suspension

But what of the employee who is alienated from her or his job? One who perceives that his or her psychological contract has been violated? The continuum outlined above may have a mirror image: behaviors which detract from or diminish role performance, and which may be assumed to damage the effectiveness of the organization. Just as there are pro-role behaviors which are presumed to be of positive intent (i.e. citizenship behaviors), there are also anti-role behaviors which may be negative in intent. To our knowledge, published research has not explored these anti-role behaviors in a coherent framework such as that of the pro-role or citizenship behavior, but rather have been more frequently examined in a fragmented fashion. However, just as pro-role behaviors can be conceptualized as ranging along a continuum from compliance to altruism, anti-role behaviors can also be arranged along a continuum. We suggest that this continuum ranges from "mere" compliance to shirking, negativism and complaints, employee theft, harassment and blocking the efforts of other employees, to even more overtly damaging behaviors such as sabotage and vandalism.

Reflecting the citizenship behaviors, we suggest that these "anti-role" behaviors can be arranged along a continuum (see Figure 8.1b), where *mere compliance* can be conceptualized as working to contract, a tactic which has long been used as a mechanism to induce work stoppages and disrupt task performance. This extreme obedience to work rules is indicative of a withdrawal of cooperation (Edwards & Scullion, 1982). *Shirking/negligence*, unlike mere compliance, involves the intentional opportunistic withholding of effort from prescribed tasks. *Negativism* includes complaining about minor inconveniences and allowing trivial barriers to impede task performance. *Theft* is the taking of resources to which one has no entitlement, including office pilferage, personal long distance calls on company phones, and embezzlement. *Harassment/threats* are characterized by anti-social behaviors directed at another individual in the organization, with the intent of impeding their task completion or causing them distress. Finally, *overtly damaging* behaviors are those which are intended to inflict substantial damage on the organization or one of its members, and would include acts such as vandalism, sabotage, and even workplace homicide.

These negative and even aggressive behaviors may be the result of frustration (e.g. Dollard et al, 1939) and injustice (da Gloria, 1984), or a feeling of a loss of control or identity. Although employees may feel entitled to certain organizational resources as understood privileges or entitlements in an equity sense (e.g. using office phones for personal calls, taking pens and pencils for home use), they may also steal as a way to get even with their employer for perceived injustices or inequities (Greengard, 1993). Employees may engage in sabotage to reduce their workload when they feel overworked (Giacalone, 1990) or in retaliation for management policies or personnel practices (Crino & Leap, 1989). These employees have reported feelings of alienation and exploitation. Employees may use sabotage as one mechanism for regaining power and control in their environments (Thompson, 1983)—a trend that is a leading cause of computer failures in organizations (Ferelli & Trowbridge, 1990).

Like the more benevolent OCBs, these malevolent behaviors are (1) voluntary, and (2) intentional. The more intense forms of anti-role behavior also share a third characteristic: (3) the intent behind the act is to damage the organization.

As depicted in Figure 8.2, pro-role behaviors are intended to benefit the organization, and are typically role expanding or enhancing. In contrast, anti-role behaviors are intended to harm the organization; required behaviors are intentionally withheld or suspended, and are typically role detracting. Between the extremes lie compliance behaviors, or behaviors which lie within Barnard's (1938) zone of indifference. Compliance behaviors conform with the role and maintain it. As the figure suggests, where role behaviors shade into anti-role (e.g. "mere" compliance) and pro-role behaviors (conscientiousness) is ambiguous, reflecting the recognized ambiguity in the literature.

What causes an employee to move along the continuum from compliance to altruism? And what causes an employee to shift from one continuum to its mirror image, moving from mere compliance to workplace violence? We hypothesize that it is the result of the nature of the relationship between the employee and employer, as well as whether or not the psychological contract between employee and employer has been kept or broken. Just how far any particular employee goes on either continuum is a function of these factors, as well as individual traits and propensities.[3]

THE MODALITY OF EXCHANGE

Employment relationships are exchange relationships, and can be characterized as contractual (Rousseau & McLean Parks, 1993; McLean Parks, forthcoming). What is the nature of these employment relationships, and what is the range of behaviors which employees contribute (or fail to contribute) to the organization in each form of exchange relationship? At what point will these contracts change and evolve? In this section of the paper, we will discuss the notion of psychological contracts, and integrate it with the continuum of behaviors which we have discussed, behaviors which range from role suppressing/detracting (anti-role) behaviors to role conforming/maintaining (in-role) behaviors to role enhancing/ expanding (pro-role) behaviors.

Organizational Contracts: The Transactional to the Relational

Rousseau and her colleagues (e.g. Rousseau, 1989; Rousseau & McLean Parks, 1993) suggest that organizational contracts lie along a continuum, ranging from the transactional to the relational. Integrating this perspective with notions of power, McLean Parks (forthcoming) delineated an organizational contract typology along two dimensions. The first dimension, drawn from the work of Macneil (1985) and

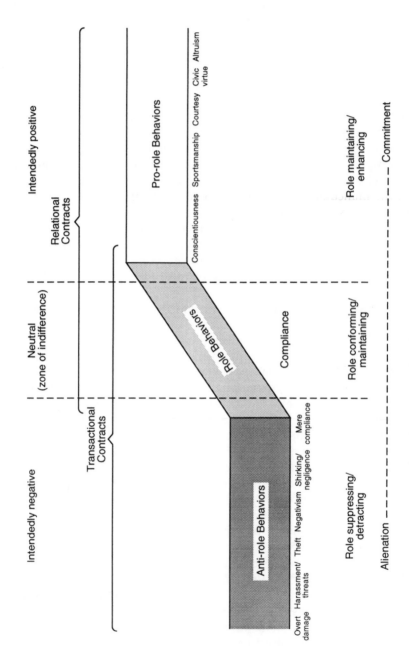

Figure 8.2 Anti-role, role, and pro-role behaviors

Rousseau (1989; Rousseau & McLean Parks, 1993), is the transactional/relational continuum. Transactional contracts are characterized by short time frames and specific obligations, in which monetizable or pecuniary resources are the primary metric of exchange. In contrast, relational contracts are characterized by long term relationships with diffuse obligations, and concerns for both pecuniary and non-pecuniary benefits. At the extreme, transactional contracts are exemplified by the "spot" contract of economics, while the extreme relational contract is exemplified by the marriage contract (Rousseau & McLean Parks, 1993). Transactional contracts are predicated on a presumption of pure self-interest, while relational contracts implicitly acknowledge the value of the relationship itself, in which one party may put the immediate interests of the other party ahead of her or his own (McLean Parks, forthcoming).

McLean Parks (forthcoming) highlights the importance of power asymmetries between the parties to the contract, in this case, organization and employee (see Table 8.1 for a summary of the typology), and argues that the explicit acknowledgement of the power relationship between employer and employee is important. She suggests that whether power is symmetric or asymmetric is likely to affect the creation, maintenance and execution (or violation) of organizational contracts. In particular, she suggests power *asymmetries* affect the perceived voluntariness of the exchange relationship, dividing parties into the broad categories of contract *makers* (relatively powerful) and contract *takers* (relatively powerless). Frequently contract takers, employees cannot easily exit the employment relationship. This may result in a perceived loss of control in the relationship, which in turn is likely to exacerbate feelings of mistreatment and injustice when violations are perceived. Feelings of powerlessness and frustration are likely to increase, arousing reactance (Brehm, 1966) or a more extreme reaction to the injustice than might otherwise be manifest. Although the employment relationship may be technically voluntary, it may be so while under a level of "duress". The more powerful party (contract maker) is able to dictate the terms of the contract to the relatively powerless party (contract taker), who must either accept its terms or exit the relationship (McLean Parks, forthcoming; Rousseau & McLean Parks, 1993).

Like most forms of economic exchange, self-interest is an underlying assumption of the transactional contract. These contracts are of short duration, their terms well specified and the resources exchanged are easily quantifiable and monetized. When power is *symmetric* between the parties, this type of contract might be exemplified by the outsourcing of computer programming by a management information systems (MIS) department, or an executive consultant—a temporary employee, but one

Table 8.1 A typology of organizational contracts

Contracting between parties of symmetric power

	Relational contracts	Transactional contracts
Motivation	"Collective" interest	Self-interest
Time frame	Open-ended or long	Short/finite
Stability	Dynamic	Static
Scope	Diffuse responsibilities	Precise responsibilities
Range of outcome behaviors	Mere compliance to altruism	Theft to conscientiousness

Contracting between parties of asymmetric power

	Relational contracts		Transactional contracts	
	Contract maker	Contract Taker	Contract Maker	Contract Taker
Motivation	"Other" interest	Self-interest	Self-interest	Self-interest
Time frame	Long	Long	Short/finite	Short/finite
Stability	Dynamic and adaptive	Dynamic	Static	Adaptive
Scope	Diffuse responsibilities	Diffuse responsibilities	Precise responsibilities	Precise responsibilities
Range of outcome behaviors		Shirking to courtesy		Overt damage to compliance

Adapted from Macneil (1985); Rousseau (1989); Rousseau & McLean Parks (1993); and McLean Parks, forthcoming.

with considerable power in the relationship. However, power may also be asymmetric between the parties. In a transactional contract with asymmetric power, the terms of the contract again are precise and well delineated. However, due to the power asymmetry, terms are extended by the contract maker to the contract taker in toto—they can be accepted as is, or rejected. The power differences endemic to this type of contract can encourage the misuse or abuse of power, and at the extreme, might be exemplified by the contract between migrant worker and land owner. Temporary secretaries are also parties to exploitive contracts—their relationship with the organization will be of short duration, and they are relatively powerless in affecting the nature or the terms of their employment contract.

At the relational end of the continuum, obligations are ambiguous and vague, and the terms may be constantly evolving. These contracts are long term in nature, and exchange not only monetizable resources, but also socio-emotional resources, such as loyalty and affiliation. An example of a relational contract with symmetric power would be the Amana Colony Woolen Mills, or the contract between the partners of law or accounting firms. However, when power is asymmetric, a normative constraint is imposed on the contract maker not to abuse the power relationship. These contracts are exemplified by the contracts between mentor and protégé, between supervisor and subordinate.

THE EXECUTION AND VIOLATION OF THE PSYCHOLOGICAL CONTRACT

We have discussed the range of behaviors available to employees in dealing with their organizations, ranging from overtly damaging behaviors (e.g. sabotage) to the overtly beneficial behaviors (e.g. altruism). The choice of behaviors in a contractual relationship is only one component of the evolution of the psychological contract (Rousseau & McLean Parks, 1993). The contract may be breached, it may be executed, or it may be renegotiated. Under what circumstances is the employee likely to comply with the terms of the contract? To go beyond its terms into the realm of pro-role behaviors? Or to engage in anti-role behaviors, intended to damage the organization? We will now turn to a discussion of the consequences of psychological contracts, in particular, when they have been broken.

The violation of a psychological contract is likely to have profound repercussions (Schein, 1980). Employees who previously were committed may withdraw. Cognitive dissonance (Festinger, 1957) will lead employees to redefine the terms of the broken psychological contract. Formerly conscientious employees may shirk; formerly dedicated employees may steal from the organization in response to a violation of their psychological contracts. Specific behaviors which have been offered by the employee before violation will be withdrawn. Citizenship behaviors will be an early casualty of a violated psychological contract, primarily because pro-role behaviors are easier to reduce or limit than prescribed activities. Organ (1988; p.78) notes, "The most salient means of redefining the contract is to with-hold those contributions [with an extra-role] character". As the employee moves from an extreme relational towards a transactional contract, behaviors that s/he contributes can move from the overtly beneficial behaviors of altruism to overtly damaging behaviors such as sabotage.

When will employees perceive a violation of their psychological contracts? A variety of events punctuate organizational life and can trigger a reassessment of the psychological contract. Employees will reassess their psychological contracts periodically in response to organizational changes (Rousseau & McLean Parks, 1993). Guzzo, Nelson and Noonan (1992) suggest economic downturns, changes in workforce composition, external environmental changes (i.e. the legal environment),[4] and management changes can all lead to a re-evaluation of the employment relationship. Wiesenfeld and Brockner (1993) suggest perceived injustice in and of itself may trigger a re-evaluation, as well as layoff announcements, work structure changes, pay rises, mergers and other personnel changes, wage freezes or paycuts, smoking bans, drug testing and the introduction of other surveillance devices, disciplinary actions, promotions and performance reviews. This re-evaluation may indicate to the employee that his or her psychological contract has been violated.

Additional demands may also precipitate a reassessment of the psychological contract and a change in employee behaviors. A grocery store employee recently justified theft as a mechanism for "getting even" in response to continually rising performance standards and perceived exploitation. The employee stated, "if you don't work *off the clock*, the job won't get done" (emphasis in the original; Greengard, 1993). Increasing and unrewarded demands (i.e. working off the clock) were "equalized" by stealing from the organization. Finally simple social comparison processes, such as comparing one's own efforts and outcomes or even employment status to those of another employee, are likely to cause a re-evaluation of the psychological contract, where the mere presence of contingent workers can reduce the core employees' trust in their employer (Pearce, 1993).

What happens when the psychological contract is violated? Robinson et al (1991) and Wiesenfeld and Brockner (1993) found that contracts become more transactional following violation. They suggest that the employee will turn away from the socio-emotional aspects and focus on the pecuniary benefits of the relationship to psychologically distance herself or himself from the source of violation, making the contract more transactional. The range of behaviors perceived by the employee as potential contributions will shift (see Figure 8.2), moving away from pro-role behaviors towards less benevolent behaviors, perhaps even into the domain of anti-role behaviors.[5] Just as pro-role behaviors are related to increased employee commitment and satisfaction, anti-role behaviors may be associated with feelings of alienation or marginalization.

How far will the employee's psychological contract shift along the continuum of behaviors in response to a perceived violation? Notions of justice will play a particularly important role, since contracts evolve to ensure fairness in exchange relationships (Ouchi, 1980) and are predicated on notions of good faith and fair dealing (Rousseau, 1989; Rousseau & McLean Parks, 1993). Research has consistently shown that perceptions of fairness and justice are important predictors of OCBs (e.g. Bies, Martin & Brockner, 1993; Moorman, 1991; Organ & Konovsky, 1989), and are quite important in determining employee reactions to employer actions. Recently, Wiesenfeld and Brockner (1993) found *procedural* justice was most important to those involved in relational contracts, while *distributive* justice was more important to those whose psychological contract was transactional. Intuitively this makes sense. The emphasis on monetized return in the transactional contract suggests an instrumental orientation, where fairness concerns will focus on outcomes or distributions. In contrast, an important component of the relational contract, with its longer time frame, is understanding that the process is fair. Although an employee may come up short in one instance or another, if procedures are fair, s/he can assume that in the long run, things will even out. McLean Parks (forthcoming) has also suggested that two other forms of justice may be important in the evaluation of the psychological contract: *interactional* justice, and *retributive* or retaliatory justice. We will briefly turn our attention to a discussion of each of these forms of justice, and their apparent relationship to relative power levels and different forms of contract.

Justice: Ensuring Fair Resolution in Contracting

Justice research has focused on two forms of justice (e.g. Folger & Greenberg, 1985), specifically *distributive* (e.g. Adams, 1965) and *procedural* (e.g. Thibaut & Walker, 1975) justice. More recently, researchers have turned their attention to *interactional* (Bies, 1987) justice; however, *retributive* justice (e.g. Hogan & Emler, 1980) has been relatively ignored. Each form of justice plays a critical role in determining employee responses to a violation of their psychological contracts.

Outcomes are Important

Both distributive and retributive justice are concerned with the fairness of *outcomes*, and consequently are likely to be associated with transactional contracts, with their emphasis on pecuniary outcomes and self-interest. Hogan and Emler (1980) noted that distributive and retributive justice reflect the positive and negative sides of justice in allocations. Distributive justice focuses more on the positive side of allocations or what one has been *given*—did I *receive* my fair share? In contrast, retributive justice focuses on the negative side of allocations, or what one has had *taken away*—what can I *take* to even the score?

The relative importance of each form of outcome justice, however, is also affected by the underlying power structure of the relationship. When power is symmetric, parties may rely on their balance of power to enforce the terms of the contract and ensure fair outcomes. However, when power is asymmetric, the powerholder may be able to dictate the distribution of outcomes. Building on Homans (1976), Hogan and Emler (1980) propose that distributive justice is an important concern of powerholders—suggesting perhaps a symmetry (or near symmetry) in the power relationship, but retribution is possible in asymmetric relationships. Specifically, although power at some level is needed to compensate for inequity (distributive injustice), "almost anyone can have revenge" (retributive injustice; Hogan & Emler, 1980).

Distributive justice is exemplified by the axiom of a "fair day's work for a fair day's pay". All forms of contracts will be concerned with distributive justice, as fair outcomes are a reason for contracting; however, distributive justice will be the primary concern of transactional contracts (Wiesenfeld & Brockner, 1993). We would predict that distributive justice would be the *most* salient form of justice in the transactional contract, especially when power is symmetric. Power between the parties is equal, so fair allocations are more likely to be ensured. Power symmetries create a situation similar to the concept of bilateral deterrence (e.g. Lawler, 1986)—knowing that one's contracting partner is equally powerful will discourage contract violations. And, if breached, the violated party will attempt to restore balance in the transaction, following the predictions of equity theory (Adams, 1965) or by attempting to renegotiate the contract. Distributive *injustice* has consistently been found to predict reductions in effort (shirking) and employee theft through pay cuts (Greenberg 1990, 1993) and even as reactions to differential status (e.g. Greenberg, 1988), in attempts to restore fairness to the relationship when one party perceives that the contract has been violated.

In contrast, retributive justice can be conceptualized as "getting even", "an eye for an eye" strategy or punishment for perceived contract violations, where the assumption is that "everyone suffers equally" (Hogan & Emler, 1980; p.134). Retributive justice, then, is related to the notion of credible threats or a "tit for tat" strategy in game theory and economics (e.g. Axelrod, 1984), where the intent is to *punish* the violator. Retributive justice is of concern to both parties: the contract maker (in our case, the *employer*) wants to inhibit contract violation, and may do so by making the consequences of violation salient and potentially painful (e.g. Leatherwood & Spector, 1991; Trevino, 1991). In this case, the *possibility* that the more powerful party will invoke retributive justice may keep the less powerful party from breaching the contract. However, retributive justice is also likely to be quite important to the less powerful party. If the contract maker breaches the contract, the contract taker will feel exploited, and may come to believe that the only recourse available to a violated contract is "getting even". In the transactional realm, we would predict that once an assessment of distributive justice has been made and found to be lacking, that in exploitive contracts, the next stage will be to assess the potential for retributive justice, possibly resorting to retribution in order to even the score.

Process is Important

Both procedural and interactional justice are focused on *process*, rather than outcomes, and consequently will be important to the parties in a relational contract. Process, in and of itself, implies longer commitments and an unfolding or a progression over time, necessarily embedding these forms of justice in the relational contract. This inclusion of time into justice considerations is important, and is a defining characteristic of the relational contract, emphasizing the importance of considerations beyond those addressed by distributive justice. As Organ (1988; p.74) notes, "[w]hat might otherwise seem criminally unjust in the short run might be absorbed without a whimper if viewed in a longer framework".

Procedural justice addresses whether or not the procedure used to reach decisions about outcomes is seen as fair. Procedural justice is focused on the perceived fairness of the decision making process that the decision maker used in arriving at a final decision (e.g. Folger & Greenberg, 1985; Lind & Tyler, 1988). These fair procedures are important over and above the extent to which they explain fairness in the outcomes (Lind & Tyler, 1988; Organ & Moorman, 1992). In contrast, interactional justice is concerned with the extent to which the actual procedures are implemented in a manner that respects the parties involved and protects their dignity (Bies & Moag, 1986; Moorman, 1991; Organ & Moorman, 1992). For example, considerate and respectful treatment would be considered forms of interactional justice.

When relational contracts are violated or breached, they become more transactional in nature (Robinson et al, 1991; Wiesenfeld & Brockner, 1993). The range of behaviors from which employees choose to contribute may shift. However, the extent and nature of this shift will in part be mitigated or exacerbated by perceptions of justice, where the justice *process* is of particular importance in the relational contract. In contracts with symmetric power, both parties are likely to have had input in the determination of the procedures through which allocations are made. Thus we would expect that procedural justice would be less of a concern. However, process is still important, and when the contract has been breached, the focus will be on interactional concerns. If outcomes deriving from such contracts are unfair (distributive injustice) then the nature of the interactions between the parties will be assessed. If found unjust, the behaviors contributed to the relationship will become more transactional in orientation. Mistreatment (interactional injustice) can be unbearable when combined with distributive injustice (Folger, 1993).

All forms of justice are likely to come into play in a relational contract with asymmetric power. If distributive injustice has been perceived, procedures become important—the contract takers, unable perhaps to directly affect the procedures themselves, must see them as fair and just in order to trust the imposed outcomes, and will make an assessment of the procedures which lead to the unfair outcome. If the process is seen as unfair, the contract taker will make an additional assessment concerning interactional justice. If interactional *in*justice obtains, the contract maker will assess the potential for retributive justice (Figure 8.3).

In sum, as suggested by Figure 8.3, we suggest that the re-evaluation of the psychological contract is a process of examining perceptions of fairness and justice. In transactional contracts the focus of attention is on outcomes. Thus, when a reassessment of the psychological contract is triggered, distributive justice will be assessed. If injustice is perceived, then the contract is adjusted by either becoming more transactional, or in extreme cases, by seeking retribution. Relational contracts, however, are focused on longer time frames and include socio-emotional resources. Thus process will also be assessed. When the re-evaluation of the psychological contract is triggered, distributive justice will again be evaluated. If distributive *injustice* prevails, then the processes of justice are evaluated. Interactional justice will be assessed in power-symmetric relationships, as it can be assumed that both parties had input into the process. However, in power-asymmetric relationships, both procedural

Transactional Contracts

Both Symmetric and Asymmetric Power

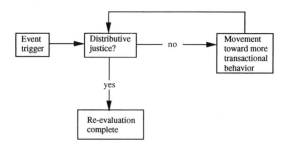

Relational Contracts

Symmetric Power

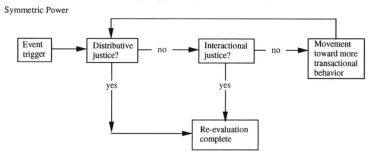

Asymmetric Power

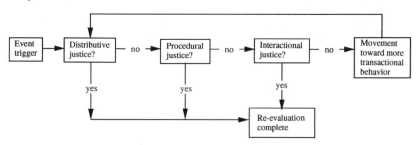

Figure 8.3 The re-evaluation of the psychological contract. Note: If perceived injustice is extreme, movement towards transactional behavior will be severe and may involve retributive justice

and interactional justice will be assessed. When injustice is perceived in the relational contract, the contract may become more transactional, or the next form of justice may be assessed. If each form of justice is found lacking (i.e. distributive, procedural, or interactional) then the results are likely to be cumulative, and reactions more pronounced. The violated party can reframe the psychological contract in more transactional terms, moving away from the pro-role behaviors, or may seek retribution, moving into the realm of anti-role behavior.

The nature of the relationship in terms of its placement on the transactional/relational continuum, as well as the relative power between the parties, will affect the process through which employees re-evaluate their psychological contracts. All contracts are concerned with the issue of fair distribution. However, if distributive injustice prevails, other forms of justice may be salient in different forms of psychological contracts. Each time an assessment is made and injustice found, behaviors will become more transactional. The process is resolved when either justice obtains (by perceiving justice or rebalancing the scales through more transactional behaviors), or when retribution is sought. The degree of injustice perceived is likely to be cumulative. Hence in relational contracts with *asymmetric* power, where numerous forms of justice are assessed, the potential movement from relational to transactional may be quite pronounced. When retribution is sought, it will include extreme movement along the transactional/relational continuum, such that the employee may move from role conforming/maintaining behaviors into the realm of extreme anti-role behaviors, such as sabotage and aggression.

CONCLUSION

We have been largely silent in our paper on three issues: (1) We have not explicitly examined the *employer* side of the contract and the inducements which are offered to the employee. Just as employees shirk, so can employers. Just as employees can jeopardize the safety of the workplace, so too can employers (e.g. failing to implement Occupational Safety and Health Administration (OSHA) standards). Just as employees can go beyond the requirements, so can employers. This side of the employment contract is also of interest, but is outside the parameters of the current paper (see, however, Kidder, 1993 for a discussion of employer responses to transactional contract behaviors). (2) We have not explicitly addressed what happens when the psychological contract is *kept*. Is the psychological contract then a continuation of the status quo? Is current behavior simply reinforced, making the contract more rigid? Does it become more relational as good will is enhanced by a kept promise? Is it ever possible to go from the very transactional contract to the very relational? (3) We have also not addressed the question of whether, once violated, a psychological contract can be healed. These are also issues of interest.

Employment contracts are changing. As a consequence, the psychological contracts of employees are also changing. The realities of downsizing and the increased use of contingent workers have been documented in academe as well as the popular press. The impact these changes have on employee behaviors, as well as the bottom line, should be of great concern to researchers and practitioners alike. Prescriptions that have worked well in the past may no longer work, and worse yet, may be perceived as manipulative and exploitive, creating a potential backlash from formerly loyal and committed employees. Research suggests contingent workers—those who accept transactional contracts—receive lower benefits and wages, and they are disproportionately young, female and minority (Russell, 1991). Temporary workers may increase organizational flexibility and decrease labor costs. However, there is a price. The price may come in terms of long-run effectiveness. The price may also include a withdrawal of pro-role behaviors, or worse, engaging in anti-role behaviors. Increasingly transactional contracts may result in decreased loyalty and employee alienation. Core workers may become overworked (Schor, 1992). These core employees may compare themselves to the contingent workers, and begin to reassess their *own* psychological contracts. Although the contracts of temporary workers are more overtly transactional, employees (such as core employees) may *perceive* their own contract as transactional, whether or not it was intended as such by the employer (Wiesenfeld & Brockner, 1993). Wiesenfeld & Brockner (1993) note, "that the psychological definition of contingent work implies that workers who view themselves as contingent have a short term outlook on their involvement with an organization because the future holds no promise for them".

We suggest worker contributions to organizations fall along a wide continuum, ranging from role enhancing behaviors (e.g. working through lunch) to compliance to role detracting behaviors (e.g. theft and violence), a continuum of varying intensity, commitment and alienation. Feelings of violation, alienation, and marginalization will contribute to the movement along the transactional/relational continuum. Employees may choose to contribute behaviors which are role conforming or maintaining, such as compliance: a behavior offered as a fair day's work for a fair day's pay. Employees whose psychological contract is relational, characterized by sentient ties and commitment, may engage in pro-role behaviors, expanding and enhancing their job roles by doing more than the minimum. Conversely, employees who are disaffected and alienated by a perceived violation of their psychological contract will become more transactional in their dealings with the organization, adjusting their behaviors to "even the score". These employees may engage in anti-role behaviors, behaviors which detract from the job role, exemplified by mere compliance, shirking, theft, or even more overtly damaging behaviors.

Current economic conditions are sparking a reassessment of the organizational structure, and new forms are emerging, quite different from the bloated bureaucracies which preceded them. The variety in organizational forms is paralleled by a variety of organizational contracts characterizing the employment relationship, contracts which range from transactional to relational, contracts in which employees may be either contract makers or contract takers. These changes create the opportunity for organizations to find a "fit" between their needs and those of their employees. In some instances, the benefits of a transactional contract and its inherent flexibility may exceed its costs. In others, the benefits of a loyal and committed worker, one who willingly engages in pro-role behaviors, will be more valuable to the organization. Future research should identify conditions under which each employment relationship is optimal, for both organizations and the employees who work for them.

ACKNOWLEDGEMENTS

This paper was written while the first author was on leave of absence from the Industrial Relations Center at the University of Minnesota and visiting at Cornell University. The authors wish to thank Ed Conlon, Jennifer J. Halpern and Denise Rousseau for their comments on earlier versions of this manuscript. The ideas presented in this paper were conceived while the first author was a Summer Scholar at the 1992 Summer Workshop on Conflict Resolution at the Center for Advanced Study in the Behavioral Sciences. The workshop was funded by the Andrew Mellon Foundation. We are most appreciative of their support.

NOTES

1. Schor (1992; p. 29) suggests these overworked Americans are averaging an additional 163 hours per year above the number of hours for employees in the previous two decades. There is a gender difference in her figures: males work 98 more hours per year, while females work 305 additional hours per year.
2. Perhaps the best example of conscientious behavior is provided by Organ (1988): Regular attendance is a contractual obligation where there are some conditions when it becomes discretionary (e.g. unused vacation days or severe weather). If employees go beyond minimum levels of acceptable attendance, they have been conscientious. Organ refers to Smith's (1977) example, where employees who made extraordinary efforts to get to work in a blizzard were conscientious—they would not have been penalized for an absence, nor were specific benefits provided for their attendance. Conscientious behavior is characterized by exerting effort on behalf of the organization beyond minimum requirements for an adequate job, but focused *towards required behaviors.*
3. These behaviors are not mutually exclusive. Employees may execute the

terms of their contracts precisely, but may steal from the organization. Similarly, employees may help other employees on their tasks (altruism) while shirking on their own task.

4. The current debate over national health is an example. If employees regard health benefits as an important inducement which they receive from their organizations and these benefits (or their costs) change as a result of changes in the healthcare system, they may re-evaluate their psychological contract with the organization with the creation of a national health plan. The North American Free Trade Agreement (NAFTA) is another case in point.

5. We have depicted the range of behaviors graphically showing a "discontinuity", to emphasize the nature of what we believe will be the movement along this range from the relational to the transactional contract. Specifically, this would be consistent with the notion that an employee has reached a particular "threshold"—perhaps a threshold of perceived contract violation or an accumulation of perceived injustices—where s/he markedly switches to another form of behavior which is quite different in nature from the previous form of behavior (i.e. malevolent as opposed to benevolent). The evolution from relational to transactional contract may be gradual, characterized by small, incremental movements when the employee perceives a contract violation. However, once this threshold has been reached, the change may be quite drastic—in the words of the immortal Popeye, "That's all I can stands, cuz I can't stands no more." As Guzzo, Nelson and Noonan (1992) suggested in the realm of commitment, examining these behaviors and the movement from the relational to the transactional contract might be best accomplished through modelling them as discontinuous and abrupt (e.g. catastrophe theory; Woodcock & Davis, 1978).

REFERENCES

Adams, J. (1965) Inequity is social exchange. In L. Berkowitz (Ed.) *Advances in Experimental Social Psychology*, New York: Academic Press.

Ansberry, C. (1993). Down the up escalator: Why some workers are falling behind. *Wall Street Journal*, 3-11-93: A:1.

Axelrod, R. (1984) *The Evolution of Cooperation*. New York: Basic Books.

Barnard, C. (1938) *The Functions of the Executive*. Cambridge, MA: Harvard University Press.

Bies, R. (1987) The predicament of injustice: The management of moral outrage. In L. Cummings & B. Staw (Eds.) *Research in Organizational Behavior*, Greenwich, CT: JAI Press, pp.83–99.

Bies, R. & Moag, J. (1986) Interactional justice: Communication criteria of fairness. In R. Lewicki, B. Sheppard & M. Baserman (Eds.) *Research on Negotiations in Organizations*, Vol. 1. Greenwich, CT: JAI Press.

Bies, R., Martin, C. & Brockner, J. (1993) Just laid off but still a "good citizen"? Only if the process is fair. *Employee Responsibilities and Rights Journal*, **6**, 227–238.

Brehm, J. (1966) *A Theory of Psychological Reactance*. New York: Academic Press.

Brief, A. & Motowildo, S. J. (1986) Prosocial organizational behaviors. *Academy of Management Review*, **11**, 720–725.

Brockner, J., Grover, S., Reed, T. & DeWitt, R. (1992) Layoffs, job insecurity, and survivors' work effort: Evidence or an inverted-U relationship. *Academy of Management Journal*, **35**, 413–425.

Church of England (1750) *The Book of Common Prayer, and Administration of the Sacraments, and Other Rites and Ceremonies of the Church, According to the Use of the Church of England; Together with the Psalter or Psalms of David, Pointed as they are to be Sung or Said in Church*, Cambridge, published by Joseph Bentham.

Crino, M. & Leap, T. (1989) What HR managers must know about employee sabotage. *Personnel*, **66**:5, 31–38.

da Gloria, J. (1984) Frustration, aggression, and a sense of injustice. In A. Mummendey (Ed.) *Social Psychology of Aggression: From Individual Behavior to Social Interaction*. New York: Springer-Verlag, pp. 127–141.

Diesenhouse, S. (1993) In a shaky economy, even professionals are 'temps'. *The New York Times*, May 16: F5.

Dillin, J. (1993) As 'good' jobs become 'bad' jobs, Congress takes a closer look. *Christian Science Monitor*, 6-18-93: 1.

Dollard, J., Doob, L., Miller, N., Mowrer, O. & Sears, R. (1939) *Frustration and Aggression*. New Haven: Yale University Press.

Edwards, P. & Scullion, H. (1982) *The Social Organization of Industrial Conflict*. Oxford: Blackwell.

Ferelli, M. & Trowbridge, D. (1990) People are the security problem, not computers. *Computer Technology Review*, **10**, 8–9.

Festinger, L. (1957) *A Theory of Cognitive Dissonance*, Stanford: Stanford University Press.

Folger, R. (1993) Reactions to mistreatment at work. In J. K. Murnighan (Ed.) *Social Psychology in Organizations: Advances in Theory and Research*. Englewood Cliffs, NJ: Prentice Hall, pp. 161–183.

Folger, R. & Greenberg, J. (1985) Procedural Justice: An interpretive analysis of personnel Systems. In K. Rowland & G. Ferris (Eds.), *Research in Personnel and Human Resources Management*, Vol. 3, 141–183.

George, J. (1991) State or Trait: Effects of positive mood on prosocial behaviors at work. *Journal of Applied Psychology*, **76**, 299–307.

George, J. & Brief, A. (1992) Feeling good—doing good: A conceptual analysis of the mood at work—organizational spontaneity relationships. *Psychological Bulletin*, **112**, 310–329.

Giacalone, R. (1990) Employee sabotage: The enemy within. *Supervisory Management*, **37**(7), 6–7.

Greenberg, J. (1988) Equity and workplace status: A field experiment. *Journal of Applied Psychology*, **73**, 606–613.

Greenberg, J. (1990) Employee theft as a reaction to underpayment inequity: The hidden costs of paycuts. *Journal of Applied Psychology*, **75**, 561–568.

Greenberg, J. (1993) Stealing in the name of justice. *Organizational Behavior and Human Decision Processes*, **54**, 81–103.

Greengard, S. (1993) Employees steal from supermarkets as a way to get even. *Personnel*, **72**, 4, 86.

Guzzo, R., Nelson, G. & Noonan, K. (1992) Commitment and employer involvement in employees' nonwork lives. In S. Zedeck (Ed.) *Work, Families and Organizations*, San Francisco, CA: Jossey-Bass.

Hart, D. (1988) Management and benevolence: The fatal falw in Theory Y. In K. Kolenda (Ed.) *Organizations and Ethical Individualism*. New York: Praeger, pp. 73–106.

Hartnett, J. (1991) A note on the People survey: EEOC data and validation of the honesty scale. *Journal of Psychology*, **125**, 489–491.

Hogan, R. & Emler, N. (1980) Retributive justice. In M. Lerner & S. Lerner (Eds.) *The Justice Motive in Social Behavior: Adapting to Times of Scarcity and Change.* New York: Plenum Press, pp. 125–143.

Homans, G. (1976) Commentary in L. Berkowtiz & E. Walster (Eds.) *Advances in Experimental and Social Psychology*, Vol. 9. New York: Academic Press, pp. 231–244.

Katz, D. & Kahn, R. L. (1978) *The Social Psychology of Organizations.* New York: John Wiley.

Kedjidjian, C. (1993) Is anyplace safe? *Safety and Health*, October, 79–84.

Kidder, D. (1993) Why aren't all jobs temporary? *Proceedings*, the First Organizational Studies. Doctoral Students Conference, Albany, NY, October.

Kidder, D. & McLean Parks, J. (1993) The good soldier: Who is (S)he? Paper presented at the 1993 Academy of Management Meetings, Atlanta, GA, and published in the *Proceedings*.

Lawler, E. (1986) Bilateral deterrence and conflict spiral: A theoretical analysis. In E. Lawler (Ed.), *Advances in Group Process*, Vol. 3. Greenwich, CT: JAI Press, pp. 107–130.

Leatherwood, M. & Spector, L. (1991) Enforcements, inducements, expected utility and employee misconduct. *Journal of Management*, **17**, 553–570.

Lind, E. & Tyler, T. (1988) *The Social Psychology of Procedural Justice.* New York: Plenum Press.

McLean Parks, J. Organizational contracting: A "rational" exchange? In J. Halpern & B. Stern (Eds.) *Non-Rational Elements of Organizational Decision Making.* Ithaca, NY: ILR Press. Forthcoming.

McLean Parks, J. & Schmedemann, D. (1994) When promises bercome contracts: Implied contracts and handbook provisions on job security. *Human Resource Management*, in press.

Macneil, I. (1985) Relational contract: What we do and do not know. *Wisconsin Law Review*, 483–525.

Moorman, R. (1991) Relationship between organizational justice and organizational citizenship behaviors: Do fairness perceptions influence employee citizenship? *Journal of Applied Psychology*, **76**, 845–855.

Nardone, T. (1993) Contingent workers: Characteristics and trends. Paper presented at the 1993 Academy of Management Meetings, Atlanta, GA.

Negrey, C. (1990) Contingent work and the rhetoric of autonomy. *Humanity and Society*, 16–33.

Organ, D. W. (1988) *Organizational Citizenship Behavior: The Good Soldier Syndrome.* Lexington, MA: Lexington Books.

Organ, D. & Konovsky, M. (1989) Cognitive versus affective determinants of organizational citizenship behavior. *Journal of Applied Psychology*, **74**, 157–164.

Organ, D. W. & Moorman, R. H. (1992) Fairness and organizational citizenship behavior: What are the connections? Unpublished manuscript, University of Indiana, Bloomington, IN.

Ouchi, W. (1980) Markets, bureaucracies and clans. *Administrative Science Quarterly*, 129–140.

Pearce, J. (1993) Toward an organizational behavior of contract laborers: their psychological involvement and effects on co-workers. *Academy of Management Journal*, 1082–1096.

Robinson, S. L., Kraatz, M. S. & Rousseau, D. M. (1994) Changing obligations and the psychology contract: A longitudinal study. *Academy of Management Journal*, **37**, 137–152.

Rousseau, D. M. (1989) Psychological and implied contracts in organizations. *Employee Responsibilities and Rights Journal*, **2**, 121–139.

Rousseau, D. M. & McLean Parks, J. (1993) The contracts of individuals and organizations. In L. L. Cummings and B. M. Staw (Eds.) *Research in Organizational Behavior*, Vol. 15, 1–43.

Russell, K. (1991) An analysis of contingent labor. *Review of Radical Political Economics*. 208–225.

Schein, E. (1980) *Organizational Psychology*, Third Edition. Englewood Cliffs, NJ: Prentice-Hall.

Schor, J. (1992) *The Overworked American*. New York: Basic Books.

Simon, H. (1976) *Administrative Behavior*, Third Edition. New York: Macmillan.

Smith, F. (1977) Work attitudes as predictors of attendance on a specific day. *Journal of Applied Psychology*, **68**, 653–663.

Smith, V. (1983) The circular trap: Women and part-time work. *Berkeley Journal of Sociology*, **28**, 1–17.

Stuart, P. (1992) Murder on the job. *Personnel Journal*, February, 72–84.

Swardson, A. (1992). In this recession, many 'employed' aren't making a decent living. *Washington Post*, 2-9-92: A:1..

Thibaut, J. & Walker, L. (1975) *Procedural Justice: A Psychological Analysis*. Hillsdale, NJ: Erlbaum.

Thompson, W. (1983) Hanging tongues: A sociological encounter with the assembly line. *Qualitative Sociology*, **6**, 215–237.

Trevino, L. (1992) The social effects of punishment in organizations: A justice perspective. *Academy of Management Review*, **17**, 647–676.

US Congress, Office of Technology Assessment. The use of integrity tests for pre-employment screening. OTA-SET-442, Washington DC: US Government Printing, Sept., 1990.

Van Dyne, L., Cummings, L. L. & McLean Parks, J. (1995) Extra-role behaviors: In pursuit of construct and definitional clarity. In B. Staw & L. L. Cummings (Eds.), *Research in Organizational Behavior*, Vol. 15, forthcoming.

Whyte, W. H. (1956) *The Organization Man*. New York: Simon and Schuster.

Wiesenfeld, B. & Brockner, J. (1993) Procedural unfairness and the psychology of the contingent worker. Paper presented at the Academy of Management Meetings, August, 1993, Atlanta, GA.

Woodcock, A. & Davis, M. (1978) *Catastrophe Theory*. New York: Dutton.

Index

Index compiled by Liz Granger

JOURNAL OF ORGANIZATIONAL BEHAVIOR

WILEY

The International Journal of Industrial, Occupational and Organizational Psychology and Behavior

EDITOR-IN-CHIEF

CARY L. COOPER,
Manchester School of
Management, UMIST,
PO Box 88, Manchester
M60 1QD, UK

ASSOCIATE EDITORS

DENISE M. ROUSSEAU
J.L. Kellogg Graduate
School of Management,
Northwestern University,
Illinois, USA

THOMAS G. CUMMINGS
Dept of Organization
Behavior, Graduate
School of Business
Administration,
University of Southern
California, USA

CONSULTING EDITORS

JULIAN BARLING

ROBERT L. DIPBOYE

JEFFREY R. EDWARDS

DANIEL C. GANSTER

JEAN HARTLEY

LEAETTA HOUGH

ARIE SHIROM

Subscribe Now...
Telephone your credit
card order on
UK/Europe:
(0)243 770400
USA:
(212) 850 6645

The *Journal of Organizational Behavior* is increasing its coverage to meet the demand of the 1990s, and aims to report and review the growing research in the industrial/ organizational psychology and organizational behavior fields throughout the world. It focuses on research and theory in all topics associated with industrial, occupational and organizational psychology and behavior including:

· Personnel selection and training
· Motivation & work performance
· Equal opportunities at work
· Job design
· Career development
· Occupational stress & organizational health
· Quality of work life
· Job satisfaction
· Organizational change
· Employment
· Job analysis
· Behavioral aspects of industrial relations
· Managerial behavior
· Organizational structure & climate

The 1994 subscription price also includes a copy of *Key Trends in Organizational Behavior*.

To receive your **FREE sample copy of the Journal** please contact:

Tracy Clayton, **John Wiley & Sons Ltd**, Baffins Lane, Chichester, West Sussex, PO19 1UD, UK
Tel: (0243) 779777   Fax: (0243) 775878